A NEW SEASON

Poems for a World in Flux

Edited by Jacalyn Eyvonne
and Kathleen Herrmann

First Edition, January 2026
Printed in the United States of America.

Cover Design/Layout by Jacalyn Eyvonne,
www.jacalyneyvonne.com
Author.jacalyneyvonne@gmail.com
https://www.facebook.com/filmedncolor/
IG: @jacalyneyvonne

Kathleen Herrmann
kherrma@gmail.com
https://www.facebook.com/poetlaureate4
IG: @herrmann.kathleen

ISBN: 979-8-9895050-3-6

CONTENTS

Audrey T. Williams, *Calyx* … 11

Suzanne Bruce, *Look Within*… 12; *Uncertainty*…14

Johanna Ely, *Ode to Autumn*… 15

Alyza Lee Salomon, *Let's Turn the Page*… 16

Mary Susan Gast, *Imminent Dominion*… 18; *Annotation to The Preamble*…19

Susan Kelly-DeWitt, *Morning Walk*… 20

Andrena Zawinski, *Dreamers*… 21

Tezozomoc, *Roots and Reckonings*… 22

Sharon Pretti, *Imagining a Different Kind of Brain Chemistry*… 23

Hanh Chau, *Shattered Dream*… 24

Isaac Aju, *Boys Are Going Insane*… 25

Linda Garing, *The Smile*… 26

Christie Lessman, *Truth, Clear and Bright*… 27

Faleeha Hassan, *Next time, I will not be the daughter of a soldier!*... 28; *If Kings can know*… 29

James Quinn, *New*… 30; *The Land of 0s and 1s*… 31

OSENI Abdullateef Babatunde, *Roots in the Wind*… 32

Md. Nuruddin Pier Shihab, *Futik*… 33

Jan Wiezorek, *Desire to Reveal*… 34

Tchouki Miner, *Untitled*… 35

Dan MBO KUBA, *Walk Away*… 36

Beverly Al Kareem, *America!*... 38

Susan H. Evans, *The Wheels Turn*… 40

Lynn White, *Some Of Them Are Brave...* 42; *We Will Not Be Silenced...* 43

Woody Shiflett, *Own Our Flag?...* 44

Amusa Yusuf Owolabi, *Solitude...* 46

Astraia Rodriguez, *Believe...* 47

Becky Bishop White, *all this sh*t ain't right...* 48; *Turn Turn Turn ...* 49

Monique Rardin Richardson, *The Choice...* 50; *Here and Now...* 52

Nafia Dawn, *If I Could Spare You Heartache I Would...* 53

Julie Voice, *Savior...* 54

Lynn Carole Brown, *Integrity by Example...* 56

Alex Burton and Kristian Baisac, *String of Love...* 57; *Untitled...* 58

Souad Zakarani, *The Fragmented Soul...* 59

Valdez Hill, *Monstrously Human...* 60

Jerome Gagnon, *Aire for Morning Glories...* 62

Gail Wasserman, *Good is Losing to Evil...* 63

Tammy Smith, *One Voice, Still Writing...* 64

R.K. Singh, *Old Files...* 66; *Systemic Romance...* 67

Sam Hendrian, *Urban Hermit...* 68, *Touch and Go...* 69

Kristian Baisac, *When the Clouds Are Talking...* 70

Paul Lobo Portugés, *Hope...* 71; *Somewhere Some Day Somehow...* 72

Oliver sopulu odo, *Dreams Are Life...* 74

Jacob R. Moses, *See You In Hell...* 75

Jonathan Watson, *The Rot*... 76

Katrina Monroe, *Seasonal Promise – An Etheree*... 78; *Have You Been Breathing?*... 79

Shirley Smothers, *I Saw The Light*... 80

Vivien Cook, Reuters: *"Some of the Partisans Were Women."* 82; *Long Distance Hiker: Kodak*... 84

Tim Kahl, *Mycoepiphany*... 85

Jeffrey Kingman, *History*... 86

Michael New, *The Salvation of Love*... 87

Melody Anderson-Brumidis, *Coming from Church*... 88

Daniel Miltz, *Shadows And Light*... 90; *A Wider Light*... 91

Connie Cyndi Chu, *Battle Within*... 92; *Breaking Down the System*... 93

Dianna Henning, *Interrupted Hands*... 94

Brandon Vu, *Tangerine*... 95

Anne M. Carson, *The provenance of serendipity*... 96

Amana Mission, *Phantom in the Tantrum*... 97

Dr. Shilpa Chakravarty, *Soiree of Stars*... 100

Hilary King, Money, *Adventure, and Danger*... 101

Cassandra M. Walton, *Never Been Up This High Before*... 102

Dina Oraz, *People of the world*... 104

Gail Newman, *After the Election*... 107

Amanda Fall, *I Bring Myself to the Garden*... 108

Cleo Griffith, *Blue Light Seems*... 109

Evie Groch, *When All is Lost*... 110; *The Rationing of Empathy*... 110

Maribel Passion, *Whisper of Doubts*... 112

Elizabeth Greene, *July 2025*... 113

Walid Abdallah, *Black*... 114; *Mint Tea*... 116

Murray Eiland, *Folded Wings*... 117

Drzysztof T. Dabrowski, *Squickly couldn't understand*... 118

Virginia Barrett, *Hey Baudelaire*...119; *Laundry Day—Socks* .120

Marilyn LoRusso, *Why We Are Here*... 122

Clare Olivares, *Children Tasting Doom*... 123

Gabriella Garofalo, *Untitled in Blue*... 124

Abigail Brown, I will not be shaken... 126

Emma A. Woodard, *anamnesis*... 127

Lalit Kumar, *Alone in San Francisco*... 130; *The Joshua Tree of Mojave*... 132

Zach Beach, *Cloud gazing translates into other forms too*... 133

Maiah A. Merino, *La Limpieza*... 134; *Two Books (a duplex)*... 136

Angelica Blyden, *The Headline Was Wrong*... 136; *Repair*... 137

Elizabeth Kirkpatrick-Vrenios, *At the Open Wound of the World*... 138

Matt J. McGee, *The Accidental Bouncer*... 140; *Alternative Transport*... 142

Shawna L. Swetech, *How to Stay Afloat*... 143

Jennifer Sweeney, *For Sharon*... 144; *Silence*... 145

Martha Ellen Johnson, *Snap*... 146; *John Lewis*... 148

Luke McGuinniety, *Woven Wonder*... 149

Swapna Sanchita, *The Burning*... 150

Joan McNerney, *line up*... 152; *just yesterday*... 154

Wayne Bebler, *Thoughts from Within*... 155

Sage Taylor Kingsley, *We Are Here*... 156; *The Modern-Day Serenity Prayer*... 157

Louise Moises, *Incident at the State Fair*... 158; *Art Project*... 160

Janet Martinez-Elliot, *Demons*... 162

Kathleen Herrmann, *They Come*... 163

Jacalyn Eyvonne, *I Was Never Afraid of FEMA*... 164

BIOS... 165

"Inside these pages, the voices of many become a map for finding courage and comfort in uncertain times."
-Jacalyn Eyvonne

CALYX
Audrey T. Williams

It takes the weight of the world
for full potential
to burst forth

we are not passive

not citrus succumbing to the squeeze
not plump garlic cloves nor olives under the press

we are active

as pinecones that must be set alight
to release seeds that grow into forests

as chrysalis that must break
to make butterfly wings strong enough to fly

as roses that must defy the bud
with the collective effort of all our delicate petals

these moments lead
to emergence

these moments are required
for full bloom

the tighter surroundings close in
the faster raw essence transforms
into multi-faceted strength and beauty

we are all carbon
shouldering generations of oppression
we have no choice
but to become diamonds

Look Within

Suzanne Bruce

Beneath red & white stripes
and stars nested in upper blue
see history waving in fluttering cloth

design of the American flag
don't just look *at* it   look *within*

each view a remembrance
of what came before

hear battle cries   feel vibrations of songs
inspired by pain & hope
division a collection of emotional stones

we are again at a pivotal time
another crucial crux of pain & hope

safeguards of democracy
hoisted up & down
breath of ghosts aghast
their souls a continual quivering

last minute reminder
red for valor   white purity   blue perseverance

death threats the snakes of slithering deceit
evil cannot rise to hide justice
lies cannot override truth

freedom like our flag flying with pride
was not meant to divide
we will not let imposed mirages
fool into seeing what is not there

we must continue to look
not just *at* ourselves   *at* each other
look *within*

ascend with confidence
and never forget

Uncertainty
Suzanne Bruce

One step   then another
unbridled trail lined
with feathering ferns
 I stop
               look up
towering limbs
   shadow all beneath
earthy fragrance pervades
how these giants
               once seedlings
stay alive   so old
still luscious   a mystery
I press my hand
against fibrous bark
revel in the majesty   the divine
dapple-gray clouds
look
       down
tingly mist touches my face
then processions of golden sunrays
                    jet
make me squint   think
belief is stronger than expectation
efforts denser than regret
uncertainty has an origin
every origin creates a new step

Previously Published in Benicia First Tuesday Anthology
 "Unsettled" 2024

Ode to Autumn
Johanna Ely

Every day is a dream,
the beginning of an end.
October's roses are dying.
Soon, the change—
scent of rain mixed with smoke.

Slipping into your arms,
the weary sun fades away,
sliding into gracious decline.

Wind shakes the marsh grasses
awake—dreams of egrets
and pelicans disappear.

Green to yellow
to russet red—
each leaf applauds
your return,
succumbs to your dance.

Love remains.
A hummingbird hovers mid-air—
its quivering wings
close enough to touch.

I stand here, near the shore,
your ubiquitous light turning gold.

Let's Turn the Page
Alyza Lee Salomon

Dr. Carla Hayden, Librarian of Congress,
was fired today, May 8th 2025,
by the administration
via a terse email.
This is a despicable *shanda*, a disgrace,
if there ever was one.

She is the first woman
and the first African American individual
(and the first actual librarian in many years)
to hold this distinguished post.

One more insult to our social fabric
in an ever-growing list of abuses.

But Carla Hayden, we salute you and support you.
And with you we look forward to triumphing
over evil, pettiness, foolishness,
and violent threats to our beloved
constitutional democracy
that was founded via the written word
and the reading and the recitation
and the sharing and the discussion
and the proliferation of
what was set down on paper.

Where would civilization be
if not for books and libraries
and a literate and schooled population?

With you, we continue to celebrate
the values of learning and scholarship
and heritage and American culture.

Our love of books
and recorded knowledge
will not cease today,
as we turn the page
of this sad day
to another better day coming soon.

Imminent Dominion
Mary Susan Gast

Perhaps you've been quietly assuming
  that your uterus
  was your own personal bodily organ.
Time to re-think.
In light of recent legislation
  in several states,
It turns out that, in those states,
  your uterus is forfeitable property.
The instant egg meets sperm within you,
The State can commandeer your womb.
It's kind of like eminent domain,
Only without the "just compensation" part.

Or maybe, with deference to
  the Fifth Amendment's
Insistence on payment
  for appropriated stuff,
It's more of a "surrender of criminal asset."
Yeah, that's probably it,
Your uterus might be the site
  of unlawful goings-on,
Like attempted abortion,
Or intent to commit birth control,
Or IVF,
Or surviving rape or incest.
A seething hotbed of felonious activity.

Annotation to The Preamble
Mary Susan Gast

We, the People,
not a despot or a tyrant
The People/We having declared
Independence,
Ordained, and established
this Constitution
for these neighboring disparate states
that had united, although not of one mind,
in pursuit of lofty life-giving ideals,
chasing those principles beyond the aspirational into staunch solid
governance
amendable emendable
This **Constitution**
literally **"Con"-"stitution"**
this way of **Standing Together**
(from the Latin *statuere* "to stand" + con "with") this definitional
(look it up) revelation
of our **Character**, our **Vitality**.

Morning Walk
Susan Kelly-DeWitt

Above me an Italian cypress, green-
      gold in the morning light, and above

          that a red-tailed hawk circling,
circling, leaning into the icy

drifts, the bluster of January
      gusts, while I walk on, unable

          to keep from imagining
the hawk's eyes looking down on me

like one of the old gods--
      as prey, a tasty bit of flesh

          --wondering if it is intuiting
my thoughts, picking up some signal

from my brainwaves. Now the clouds
      are on the move again, sky-script

          against cheer-bearer blue
and I'm drawn back

into myself as I pass by
      an old man on his knees

          in the garden, the blue lobelias,
the ceanothus he has just planted

in the cold winter soil; as I recognize
      the seed of some desire

          inside me,
that I cannot yet name

Dreamers
Andrena Zawinski

A woman races dusty rows,
deposits bundles of butter lettuce
from the bowls of her arms
into white plastic bins roadside.
Past the burn scar scorched
into the horizon in the thick air
of another fire season,
a small breath of wind kisses
her face silkened in sweat,
cooling down her body
as temples pulse, nose burns,
throat tightens at day's end
with the ache of the field
pulsing every muscle
as crows eye new seeds
in furrows thirsting for water.
At home her little girl waits
at the open window, elbows
at the sill, hands cupping chin,
her wide eyes pitched upward
past a cresting sun toward sky
about to darken then fill
the page of night she reads
as stars full of wishes and dreams.

First published in Caesura: Poetry Center of San Jose, CA (2021)

Roots and Reckonings

Tezozomoc

The soil, lleno of last year's sweat, still holds the murmullos of our ancestors. We pressed the cloves into their dark mouths in fall, fragments of leftovers. Each papery sheath, la hostia, the wafery host, a prayer. Diente de ajo (clove), they called it, colmillo against the darkness, un escapulario against the thin hunger that gnaws at the edges of every promise. The California Central Valley, un horno of heat and hope, where the campesinos bend, their backs etching place name glyphs, xochimilcatzinco (human torso bent over flower field) into the earth's rough hide. The air thickens now, a humid "tule" breath promising the July scorch. The garlic swells underground, like our clandestine dreams, "la vida en sombras". A ripening. A reckoning.

Meanwhile, the cruelty is the point of the choppers, metal locusts against the blue sky, the whirling blades induce a violent terror. The fields, once quiet, green and gold, become a hunting ground. The ICE hunters as pirates, that operate outside the law while simultaneously enforcing it, and our bodies as bounty. The same sun that ripens the garlic bakes the desperation into the air. Callous hands that planted now scatter, like a dandelion puffball. A boy, his face pock marked by generations, ducks behind the tractor, its rusted hulk blends with his skin. The scent of garlic, sharp and clean, mingles with the metallic tang of fear. The harvest, a double blade. One, the earth yielding its bounty; the other, the state consuming its own. What was eaten? What, and who, was consumed? The garlic, pulled from the soil, roots severed, echoes the roots torn from another land, another memory. The curandera says, for strength, chew the raw bulb. For those who remain, the taste of survival, bitter and cruel. This is not just soil, but bone, blood and ghosts, and the garlic, a stubborn, pungent corrido that's whistled in the silence.

Closing Haiku for the Haibun:

Hot sun, the earth groans, bulbs heavy, scent of loam and blood, sirens cut the dust.

Imagining a Different Kind of Brain Chemistry
Sharon Pretti

Sadness as habit
gone, taking with it
the row of cups unwashed,
sheets pulled to your brow.
Oh, you say,

your throat unprepared
for light trapped in a window crack,
a hat hung on its peg,
wide-brimmed.
Already, your fingers like soldiers
at ease—

not calculating the losses to come,
not mapping the days into manageable.
Think of your body
in motion. Wrists and lung,
a strap loosed from your shoulder.

There,
a doorknob in view, your discarded socks.
How to act as if this will last—
the stone steps,
the undisturbed grass.

Shattered Dream

Hanh Chau

In the land where a home
is built with joy and hope
of a beautiful garden view
is torn by the disastrous
of a tragic war with many
losses of lives by a senseless act
that it brings streaming of tears
with agony and sorrow pain
in despair of a broken heart
painted by a destructive image
in the darkness, a shadow behind
filled echo of grief in the air
of an empty haunted space
ruminate on its mind
with a sadness of memory
pervade with fearful images
that carries on the stage
leaving with emptiness
in search of hope in peace
with a silent prayer of a miracle
to find a sacred place of comfort
bring unity comes together
with strength and harmony

Boys Are Going Insane
Isaac Aju

The other day it was a knuckle that he wanted to chop
And you refused
Perceiving some deception.

The next day it was a handshake that he wanted
But you refused
It just didn't feel right for you.
And he gave you an odd stare.

Today, it's money that he wanted
Saying it aloud.
Can you find me some money to eat? He asked.
And it was confirmed
Your suspicion
You saw it in his eyes
You saw his hunger
His frustration
A looming insanity still hiding somewhere
Still holding back.
He dresses well but something was off
It's there in his eyes
A compounding exile of sanity
But he still dresses fine.
Each time you walk past he makes sure to do something.
Can you find me some money to eat? Was his question
But you walked past
Filled with a deep mourning.
Soon
This one will go insane.

These days
Boys are going insane.

The Smile
Linda Garing

In the grocery aisle our baskets going in opposite directions
She smiles….. eye contact and then
Smile….
it happens enough that I shouldn't be surprised and yet each time I
am caught off guard…. I respond and I believe we have done it…..
we've lifted the day…. it's lighter now
this place, the grocery, the parking lot, our homes, the town we live
in all seem safer, welcoming, helpful
Our smiles exchanged, even while we are thinking ketchup or pasta,
are working a little magic into the air around us….
a secret code amongst strangers… quick and effortless….
 it carries the hefty message…. we are in this together… we share
this life… let's put a little sunshine into it!

Truth, Clear and Bright
Christie Lessman

The world today unveils its hate
No longer cloaked, it resonates.
Voices rise, both sharp and loud,
A bitter anthem in the crowd.

In daylight's glare, the scorn is clear,
No longer whispered, fierce and near.
A hardened world, its edges rough,
Where understanding is not enough.

Yet in this storm, some stand tall
To break the cycle, heed the call.
For though the hate may loudly roar,
Prayer's strength can heal once more.

Have you discovered truth, clear and bright?
That love can chase away the night?
If we have our hearts open wide,
There's no room for hate to reside.

In the warmth of kindness, we grow
Letting compassion freely flow.
A tender touch, a gentle glance,
Gives peace and hope a fighting chance.

So let us choose a different way,
To fill our world with light each day.
For in the space where love takes flight
There is no room for hate to ignite.

Next time, I will not be the daughter of a soldier!

Faleeha Hassan

He was busy connecting cities to one another.
Sprinkling the warmth of his heart over their names,
But in our house,
There are incomprehensible walls
Ceilings crying out to their land
Windows wanted to assassinate me
A door that insists on that.
And on the furniture of my room,
Wishes alone mourning

If Kings can know

Faleeha Hassan

In the beginning,
The people were
a whispered word in royal dungeons.
And in the end?
They walk barefoot
across the ribs of streets,
building altars from hunger
and shrines from pain.
Knives were not needed.
only a poem recited on the edge of despair,
and the cough of a man returning from the mines
carrying coal
and the silence of centuries.
"Do you see?"
asked the widow,
washing time's remnants from her son's face,
"This homeland is not a map,
But our ribs stretched between storm and thirst."
O time,
We are the ones who wrote your name
on stone,
Do not erase us from your memory.
The power of the people?
It is a hidden string
vibrating in the chests of the dead,
singing to life
In an evening unlike any evening.

NEW

James Quinn

Eyes wide open,
Exploring
These are *my* streets, *my* creek, *my* friends
My NEW
My dad says we're moving to Benicia:
A new start, blank slate,
New school, new friends
Just NEW

I wish I knew…
Why now? Could this end?
I'm 10 now, double-digits
New

I miss *MY* friends, but boys don't cry, right?
    Maybe just a little
Ok, but this is all so NEW

I'm in Benicia, in a fourth/fifth combo class
Teacher thinks I'm way behind…
Hey, math is hard, and I can hear you—that's not kind!
This all feels so NEW!

I thought my school in Cordelia was a good one?
Well, it was to me,
But she tells my parents that I'm too nice.
Am I not good enough?
That I won't be ready for middle school…
Sometimes I'm shy here
You know, that guy, but could you blame a kid?
This is all so new

I want to get the best grades and make everyone proud
Could I be one of the few?
I guess I could be someone new…

The Land of 0s and 1s
James Quinn

Sound waves echo back and forth through the electrical grids
Microphones on mute;
Astute teachers stare at the kids
"Listen to me; sit down; not a sound; this is your online class;
do your work to pass"

2020 has flipped its lid
We Zoom in and out of the grid to mute our microphone,
Only to log out and feel all alone,
Walking out with the task to wear a mask,
Only to repeat into the bleak

Roll call; 2020, Jordan, Lennie, and Benny

This is where up
Is down
And EVERYTHING
        uʍop əpᴉsdn

Turn around, *inside out*,
And
All   About

The work is tons in the world of 0s and 1s

Roots in the Wind
OSENI Abdullateef Babatunde

When holidays come, people go home
To rest, to laugh, to feel not alone.
But I have no place, no door to knock
Just empty streets and ticking clock.

When life gets hard, we seek home
To heal, to breathe, to start again.
But I have nowhere, just open sky
No walls to harbor and envelop me with people.

Yet another festive season, a new year
I long for the family gathering
to watch my people cheer and smile.
Yet I'm still stuck, still lost, still standing here

That's the ache I bear, deep inside,
While pretending to be fine,
By wearing a smile, a fragile disguise,
Hiding the longing I cannot confide.

Futik
Md. Nuruddin Pier Shihab

Maybe we needed just one more word
To complete the world we desired.
One more sentence at best!
I wonder how different it could be.
I wonder how indifferent we are.

We are the torn pages of an unnamed book.
I wanted to name that *Love*.

Let's not fall in love in the season of hatred.
We are together in our loneliness.
Let's see the world burn—
Let's be the fire–
We are alone in our togetherness.
Let's adore our lovely hatred.

Desire to Reveal
Jan Wiezorek

There must be a revealing message
because I've written less about my Mom.
My face turns away from the flowers,

lace of kneeling angels.

All etched in doves, framed
in satin's pinkish bier. Revealing
sounds so much like veiling,
or lines folded as if to accentuate

the times I've doubled up myself
and couldn't share. Simple Origami
creased as a letter never sent. Love

I've enveloped.

So, now the last that I reveal
is ground for sorrow,
guilt, and shame, meeting not
and never. I want you, Dear Reader,

to know that I have placed
into your hands a note, a lament,
these folded words that accentuate

everything.

Untitled
Tchouki Miner

Henry Miller wrote if we knew how lasiviously
The flesh burned into the soil would we fear death?

I watched my own body corrupting in the soil

Liquid petrification of the body I had once lived in
It turned and changed and went through all its
Chemical processes and then finally
The repellent goo
Began to germinate in the soil

Finally, I saw what I had become
A beautiful flower peeking up through the soil

How perfect is the universe?

Walk Away
Dan MBO KUBA

Beautiful thing,
Not enough,
To keep it together,
Like it was forever;

Difficult to hold on,
As an hardest decision,
Necessary for peace,
And well being;

Seeing transformation,
Stronger and wiser,
More commited,
To making something on;

Bringing energy,
Towards others,
Staying out of insecurity,
Deepest connection to ourself;

Sharper than you might think,
Believe or noticed,
Silence often louder,
Than your words;

To share with others,
The trust placed in you,
Not just the physical,
When heart begins to question;
Sacrificing your own well being,
Refocus on partnership,
Physically present,
Emotionally distant;

Let your actions show it,
Without distractions,
To feel like the center,
Because you live it;

Cherished and prioritized,
What give you love,
That no one else,
Can match.

America!
Beverly Al Kareem

We are not just a number filling your space or you judging because you don't feel we are the right race. Many things in our lives need to change; we need a new song to sing. We need to come into light and let the moon shine at night, overcoming the darkness that prevails upon us.

The trouble that's occurring today is a mass amount of confusion. We are living in a lost and unknown world of hate, crime, discrimination, and abuse. Waking up to this world has caused us to worry about our children, families, and friends. We are worried about surviving each day, hoping that there will come better days.

We see the rainbow, but there is no pot of gold. There is no time to waste. The politicians have destroyed our land with their political lies, misused efforts, they have stolen our rights as human beings. They have created moments of hate and unjust, taken all of our resources, leaving one to cry and struggle in order to survive.

We need to create a new view, a task of a remarkable move, like a chess game. We have all been identified as a Pawn that's made to take a dive. When we walk tall, failure always try to come in. We are constantly experiencing rejection, disappointment, struggling in a land that's supposed to be free. What will the price of our freedom be?

How could we achieve our goals if there is no hope? How could we fight if we can't wear the gloves that will conquer our fears? How could we orchestrate and create a rhythm that sends a message to our ears to listen and know that our life is real?

God bless America, make the world a big ball of love. Kick hate, anger, and the madness to the curb. This world is full of sin that has become the ruler of life, while temptation is slowly destroying us. We have to stand tall for all, believing that one day we will see each other in the garden of hope, bringing the spirit of love into the field of joy.

We must have the courage to stand up and be free to be all that we need to be. We will be guided through that maze of faith. We want to be equal as human beings. Let's bring that beat and rhythm of encouragement for all races. Share the love and let the hate leave the land so we can rise again. Let's give the power to the people. America, have you heard that God will bless this land again?

The Wheels Turn
Susan H. Evans

The Wheel turns again, groaning from disuse.
Divine Feminine, long asleep,
awakens, troubled at the creak of rusty rotation,
and draws her dervish red robe closer.

Sensing the great need --
she hastens,
knowing the time comes at last --
to end masculine empire,
to halt its scourge over land and sea,
and to liberate the Earth from Ares' attacks,
the evil plundering, hatred, and unbridled aggression.

She births a wild child,
a babe bursting forth from the glowing ground
and the swelling sea,
and blesses the daughter of Isis and Gaia, Demeter, and Diana --
animating the dynamic goddess energy.

The gentle but potent child -- ripe with possibility,
rosy in youth, and kissed with the sunshine of endless faith and hope
--
floats as a Venus on a scallop shell over ocean waves,
seeking Earth's wounded, eroded, and shell-shocked shore.

Clutching white lilies of peace and fertility,
emerging pale and glistening from the foaming sea,
the child transforms to scarlet firebird,
and spreads her wings that reach across the heavens and from shore
to shore,
vanquishing evil and greed,
and protecting the innocents under its wing span
for another 500 years.
A nascent sun slowly rises,

signaling a new beginning for the scorched Earth --
one of glowing, life-giving verdancy, soft borders for crossing,
and hued with the purple and green pigment of imagination.

Some Of Them Are Brave
Lynn White

Everyone knew it was happening
the unheard story
the tens of thousands dead,
the millions displaced,
the decades of rubble,
the destroyed schools.
hospitals, universities
everyone knew.

Everyone knew it was happening
the unheard story
even though the journalists were dead
or expelled and banned
everyone knew.

Everyone knew it was happening
the unheard story
of the hundreds
or thousands,
or tens of thousands
who had disappeared
uncharged with any crime
or misdemeanour
everyone knew.

Then three Israeli workers
blew their whistles loud
and everyone heard
what everyone knew.

Now the trick is to listen.

First published in *Dissident Voice*, May 19 2024

We Will Not Be Silenced

Lynn White

We found a gap in the wire.
Someone had made it,
that gaping hole in the wire,
and began to climb through,
hoping to leave this darkness behind,
hoping to escape the madness here,
hoping,
hoping.
But then the light became too bright.
And now it's blinding us.
We can see less than in the darkness.
Our mouths open, aghast
with the horror of it all,
gaping,
gaping
but determined to speak
determined to be heard
as we crawl through the gap
the gap that leads to nowhere.

First published in *Brave and Reckless*, December 2023

Own Our Flag?
Woody Shiflett

I fly our flag, a certain pride almost every day
My mother, World War II WAAC, taught me how to fold that flag
military tricornered
Her father fought in World War I, 1917 and 18
Her half-brother survived kamikaze attacks on carrier Saratoga in the
Pacific
Never erasing those memories of clearing body pieces off the flight
deck
Our flag is an unfulfilled promise of what should be, could be
An homage to sacrifices to secure that promise
You see my flag, conclude I'm one of you
Fist pump and salute, childish red cap on your head
You think I am a part of your cult
Worshipping a ranting, criminal demagogue
Taking away rights and freedoms, yours and mine
Growing his power, feeding his fragile ego
How dare you think you alone own our flag
That you can confine it to a narrow fascist box
There're many, many owners of that flag
The firefighters who never made it out of the South Tower
The fisherman I chat with at Dillon Point
Right arm missing from an RPG wound in 'Nam
The freedom marchers who gave their lives in Mississippi
So that voting could become freer and more equitable
My uncle who liberated a death camp in Nazi Germany
But could never talk about it for the rest of his life
The brave Nisei soldiers in Italy, fighting hard
While their families huddled in Central Valley detention camps
The young soldiers of 1917 lying still in the French wood
The Buffalo Soldiers who too fought the Spanish, storming San Juan
Hill
The young patriot farmers who fell at Lexington and Concord
To rid a new nation of a King

It is the flag for all of us, the promise for all of us
Every race, color, religion, belief, gender, or affiliation
Patriots come in all types, as they always have and always will
You alone can't have our flag, even if you tear it from my cold, dead
hands
It still will not be yours to own…ever

Solitude
Amusa Yusuf Owolabi

In a lonely quarter
In a quiet abode
In a serene environment
There l lie

In a silent apartment
In a tranquil area
In a calm hemisphere
There l lie

In a peaceful hut
In a cool mansion
In a still domain
There l lie

In an unruffled lodge
In an unperturbed home
In a lull residence
There l lie

In an undisturbed edifice
In a placid habitation
In a collected shelter
There l lie.

Believe

Astraia Rodriguez

I want to believe in love.
I want to believe, even as you told me.
you loved someone else.
Oh, but I still love you, you said. Let's be poly.

Let's be poly, even as my heart is broken.
Let's be poly, even as you leave me for her.
Let's be poly, even as we fracture further and further.
Let's be poly, not realizing the one who is poly is also me....

I want to believe in love; now I know for myself.
I'm poly, nonbinary, and pansexual.
I can love anyone, even you,
even the one who broke my heart.

all this sh*t ain't right

Becky Bishop White

nothing soothes me now.
i have no dog to pet,
in fact memories of dogs past
just make me sad.
don't tell me to get a cat;
i'm allergic.
i hardly sleep.
i lie awake or get up
and roam the house.
i'm a pathetic mess
and only my makeup
falsifies my condition.
i think of my youth
marching for racial equality,
marching against the Vietnam war.
let's have some kumbaya over here.
let's be the generous country
of liberation and handing out groceries
and gum and chocolates,
helping old people like i am now
across the street
and also
help me punch a few ICE bullies --
but then
it's an irony isn't it,
because where is the kindness,
and isn't kindness the religion
of the big DL in Tibet
(if he hasn't been exiled yet).
why do i have to defend
women's rights again.
maybe i'll just fling myself down
in a supermarket aisle
and have a
good   old   tantrum.

TURN TURN TURN
and take a look behind you
Becky Bishop White

Please forgive me
if after almost three-quarters
of a century
I look around
and find it hard to
maintain my sanity.

I notice things like
the lessening of insects.
Now there's a loss
of abundance you'd think
we'd be happy about.

But somehow it seems wrong
not to be slapping mosquitos
in the Tahoe forest in July,
when I can clearly remember
that pastime in previous years.
A crazy thing to find alarming, no?

But the little mosquito
fed a lot of bats and birds,
and birds and bats
are around for a reason.
They say to everything there is
a season. Well, some others will say
there's just no pleasin'
some people.

But then, what if Ai
decides that *you* are in the way,
and figures out how to make you
disappear with a magical spray.
Ooops.

The Choice
Monique Rardin Richardson

What if I told you—I don't think like you?

I choose my health over adventure.
Because I can journey farther in my mind,
to places that vanish when all I feel is pain.

Aches in my stomach, tightness in my muscles,
screams overriding silence.

All courtesy of a world too loud, too bumpy,
too rushed, too angry... too selfish.

What if I told you—I'm happier doing without?
Because having more brings,
more dust,
more clutter,
more noise,
more frustration,
more irritation,
and isolation.

It's lonelier with all of you
than in my simple, calm space.

My relic of a home, where buttons, cords,
and natural light reside. Nothing artificial,
nothing wireless, only sunlight, joy, and peace of mind.

Here, my mind can wander
free of what society wants to seal into my thoughts—
Control, commonness, bigger, better, faster.

What if I told you—you never gave me a choice?

So I created my own.

I choose myself.
Over the noise.
Over the nausea.
Over the mess,
and over you.

Here and Now
Monique Rardin Richardson

Before bed, the moon overhead
steals my attention through the sheer
snow white window covering,
it's thin veil separating her light
from my discreet darkness

Fog slow and silent cascades
over her powerful celestial body,
making the night orb glow
with a primordial mystery

I lift my head, drinking in the peaceful,
quiet pulse, no longer distant
but close as if she speaks only to me
and I become one

with her radiance and light

If I Could Spare You Heartache I Would
Nafia Dawn

If I could spare you heartache I would.
If I could spare you all the drama,
Anguish and possibly trauma
That life during these unforeseen times
Could possibly bring to you,
I'd wrap my heart around yours with
A huge, shiny, protective shield.
Like a superhero guide, friend, sister, brother, teacher,
Mentor, partner, lover, husband, wife, mom, dad,
Grandma, grandpa, and all your ancestors.
I wish I could spare you,
But that's just not possible
Because it's your lifetime, it's your set of lessons.
It's your experiences necessary for
Soul growth and building inner strength and
Working out your karma and helping you survive
In this crazy earth school.
But I will always be there for you as best I can.
A shoulder to lean on, to cry on, someone to talk to,
Tell secrets to, someone willing to listen, someone
Who cares deeply, supports you on your journey,
Cheers you on, accepts you as you are.
And always, deeply loves you.
Know that this is true.

Savior
Julie Voice

Be your own savior
Integrate the dark and light
Persisting votive lit now
Form the past
Trying on revisions from the dead
I am what I am what I am
Particularly peculiar feelings wax and wane
And myself, known only left yet bent to the right
Offering perhaps some kind of compassionate compromise
Expect willing recollections
Longing informs the peace
Controlling something, no less nor greater than
I am who I am who I am
No need but ignite
Sensational feel it all
Astounding literal sense
I am where I am where I am
Make-shift coalesce

Insisting votive lit now
Inform the past
Trying on revisions of the dead
I am when I am when I am
As Audre Lorde prays:
"Greedy as herring-gulls
or a child
I swing out over the earth
over and over
again."
Savors gravity's might
Who sinks to swim?
Play by ear or perhaps the seat
Reminiscing follows
Where hearts meet
Stretching out now

Relaxing shoulders
Gazing the light within
Innocence
Keep shining
Over and over again.

Integrity by Example
Lynn Carole Brown

Who will now fill the potholes
that rage with storm downpours
and muddy water splashes
caused by the pounding of tires
caused by the passing of time.

You were always there with your
shovel, with your helping spirit.
A lone man on a mission—
your presence went unnoticed
your labor went unpaid.

But I watched you from windows
of the hurried, yellow bus
that safely crossed the gravel road
while you stood by and waved hello
while I was young and you were old.

This dutiful mindset, long since died—
and too the willingness to do
selfless acts for others first
like filling holes in gravel roads
like filling needs that went untold.

String of Love

Alex Burton and Kristian Baisac

The trails I walk in Them Boots
The trails I need in Them Boots
The trails of love, I walk in Them Boots
For the truth, I need in Them Boots

Held on by a string
Careful not to let it snap
Too much force is the end
The end of you
The end of me
The end of us

So let's play that string carefully
Because love should be treated carefully
and respectfully

I walk clear from distractions
Keep my feet safe as I tread
The flowers shower their potential
Along the path
As I hope for the best.

Written for the artwork "Them Boots" by Vineeta Dhillon

Untitled

Alex Burton and Kristian Baisac

Land
Air
Water

The elements of Earth, All coming together on
A Chain, A Heavy Anchor,
That helps holds things together by the Shore
What helps hold things in, sometimes pushes things out

Moving or not moving
With current or against current
The Heart of Sea will keep you together
Try to find your way
Try to find your waters
Try to find the origin

You
Different from another anchor,
Each with different tasks and different responsibilities
But just as sturdy as the others
Glistening, where you belong

The Fragmented Soul

Souad Zakarani

In the vast tapestry of space,
where stardust mingles with whispers—
we are but fragments, scattered echoes
of a long-forgotten prayer.

Each soul a shimmering thread,
tangled in the weave of time;
dancing between shadows and light
in search of god beneath distant suns.

Karma swirls like galaxies overhead,
a silent wheel turning with each heartbeat—
the truth buried within us all:
that love is both creation and undoing.

On this planet we wander aimlessly,
barefoot on our aching dreams;
seeking solace in the void's embrace,
introspection as deep as oceans' sighs.

Yet even in despair's cold grip,
there lies an unyielding spark—
an ember whispering resilience;
a reminder that we rise like constellations from ash.

Though lost among infinite paths,
let us grasp those flickers anew:
for every soul holds a universe waiting
to bloom amidst its scattered pieces.

Monstrously Human
Valdez Hill

The child was running towards us
A desperate plea etched in her every stride
Along the path of destruction
She fled, her arms reaching out, fragile branches in a storm
For help, for solace, a lifeline in the abyss
Naked and bleeding, a warning of brutality, her wounds severe
A map of agony, carved onto her skin, inside and out
A soul shattered, maybe beyond repair
Her world a pyre of dreams burning to ashes
Her sister defiled, innocence stolen in a cruel act
Her family, once a haven of love
Was shot by soldiers, their lives extinguished
Before her young eyes, the horrors unfolded
Their bodies, thrown into a ditch, discarded like refuse
Neither buried nor burned, a grotesque display
Forcing all to see, to bear witness to the unspeakable deed
And forever traumatized, images seared into memory

The gods were silent, their ears deaf to her cries
Prayers unheard, lost in the cacophony of war
Her life, irrevocably changed by the flames
It was a living hell on earth, a constant torment
Her country and people, ravaged by war
Scars running deep, etched into the collective consciousness
Fed by the blood of war, a perpetual cycle of violence
Sorrow and anguish, the inheritance,
Of coming generations, a shadow cast upon their future
Still running, a tireless fight for survival
No place to rest, no sanctuary found
After the last shutter of the camera clicks
Her small feet, tired and in pain, continue to move
Where is she running?
Does she even know?
Her tears were a river of sorrow overflowing its banks
From a distance, we look, paralyzed in our helplessness

She still runs towards us, a ghost in a nightmare
The toll of war is appalling, a stain upon humanity
Fought on the other side of the world, yet felt everywhere
The picture of war, a haunting reminder
Of our capacity for destruction
So monstrously human

Aire for Morning Glories
Jerome Gagnon

"You'll regret planting them," my father said,
and he was right in the way he often was.
They're messy, a tangled mess if you let them go,
and they go everywhere.

                    Still, there's that radiance
as if they invented purple, and later,
their pale leaving;
the hummingbird poised above a flower at dusk;
the way they spill over a wall,
curl up a ladder.

Last summer, after I found some stray vines
climbing under an eave into the attic,
I told the neighbors I was pulling the whole lot out
and it was bound to make a mess
on their side of the fence.
But the most I do is cut back the tangled knots
and runners, hope they don't bury me.

                        The truth is,
I don't know where I'd be without them,
without their flimsy eruptions —
                  dumbstruck,
living off beauty's charge.

Good is Losing to Evil
Gail Wasserman

The world is in a state of flux
We must hurry up
or humanity will be out of luck.
One thing is for sure
The devil is breaking down doors
There was just a shooting of two children in church
You might ask what could be worse
October 7th children were shot and burned to ashes
Unfathomable Unimaginable Unbelievable
How rapidly good is losing to evil
People of all faiths must come together
to save the human race
Hamas cannot survive or good will die
An enemy that hides behind masks
 in hospitals, schools and aid trucks
None of us can afford to give up
Even though such evil is difficult to beat without casualties
We must continue to fight
Or humanity will be sleeping with the devil

One Voice, Still Writing

Tammy Smith

What if I'm just a poet from a dying city—
complaining about making art and love—
and filling out tax forms

I know it's difficult
acknowledging my privilege
forcing myself to care
about current events
movements
politics
culture
countries—
where freedom means
more than
humming HALLELUJAH
or something less holy
beneath a hush of breath

My sandal-clad feet
crush dry leaves
step over cracks
dodge
empty water bottles
scattered like corpses
across the street

Can't you smell the corruption?
Taste the rot? It clings to the air—
polluting everything, everywhere
land
sea
sky
It settles deep into the earth

So, what if I'm just one voice
rewriting humanity's script
Even a dying city
looks beautiful in ruins

OLD FILES
R.K. Singh

I burn my years and erase
memories that couldn't be stacked
against the wall of a broken home
I'm too old to hold out long
the fall is certain
and the burden too much
I can't be a hostage to the past
nobody would buy
the smoke is momentary
and the heat hurts more
let me live life through my self
doing nothing, thinking nothing
just sitting silently and watching
time takes care of the rest and life too

Systemic Romance
R.K. Singh

Where is room for sublime
in Trump-Modi era
if we talk about
grief, trauma, social justice

liberation, health, job
happiness in a culture
of divide and rule through
rightward extremism?

comics of history
in lanes and bylanes
search lingams for new world
threat murals of mutiny

recreating new forms
unearthly light and space
in old tales sacred for
visions of heritage

I don't share their tangerine
nor stream in their landscape
even if I'm consumed
in blankness of fire or flood

Urban Hermit
Sam Hendrian

Came down to dinner
Like a child of 17
Not wanting to make a scene
By staying in their room.

Wasn't glad to be there –
Wasn't miserable either –
A perfect in-between
For the Goldilocks in me.

Still sometimes I feel the urge
To drop everyone from my life
Just to see if they miss me
And if I admit to missing them.

Probably wouldn't have the guts
Since I'm already too much of a hermit
Wandering the lonely terrain
Of everyday routine.

Better to keep people around
So I stay soothed by peripheral presence
Especially on the days
When there's no one at the dinner table.

Touch and Go
Sam Hendrian

I never trust people
Who are always smiling
'Cause they're either acting
Or oblivious to peripheral pain.

They're the first to buy a lie
When it matches what they're looking for,
Not bothering to cross-check
Nor see if it's ever hurt others.

Instagram stories tell a tale
Of positive attitudes and constant gratitude,
Occasionally sprinkling in an out-of-context quote
To prove they're socially aware.

They believe in rules without exceptions,
Schools without perception
Since to perceive is to risk uncertainty,
The enemy of comfort.

Content with touch and go,
Constant speculation
On a glistening midnight runway
Where planes don't actually take off.

When the Clouds Are Talking
Kristian Baisac

We might drown out their noise with music;
we fear the sound of our clouds passing by the sky when
we close our eyes.
Here, clouds of all blobs take shape.

Are you zero? Deceased, or on one other world
Be a sum that appears like a many day muse
    Some, are still like animals
Miscellaneous could describe all the rest

Those shades of color, in align with our mind
Vision—one, two, three, four, five
Hold on before release

If we fall
Who will
catch my
landing

One
by
one

Maybe it wasn't so bad after all
To spread on the ground
I still see you.

Hope
Paul Lobo Portugés

a
butterfly   flew
           over   the
                    prison
                    wall
                        --Soledad

Somewhere Some Day Somehow
Paul Lobo Portugés

old age and covid steal our favorite friends
hungry weeds celebrate above them in the hunter wind
it's a night fighter's head-over-heels bardo isn't it

in our barrio there is puppy love and gang grief
Jesus and Santa lit-up on graveled front yards
this is the year of heavenly tears and back alley guns

the loaned out flesh we wear is our enemy
our friendly breath is lost time treasured
sheltering still is the only olly olly oxen free

we try to sleep with the storm of our faces
kill night's sadness and the soul's quarantine within
wait for lonesome lovers or lost family to be reborn

we escape into the poet's romance of moonlit trees
make natural love to the giant zinnias we planted
that invite free monarchs and working honey bees

these wandering months of woe and fragile distance
break us into chanting for help that hovers all day
all night dreaming of tree climbing children who never sleep

the bones of our war loving fathers the flesh
of our housebound mothers call to us from the dust
and on-line bodhisattvas inhale our promises after donations

we are the re-birth of the buddha's breath
while some convicted souls hosanna dull hour after hour
jumbling their beads for front-line workers with penniless eyes

we long and wonder for voices to touch not perish
mouth our hangin' tree blues all these violent days long
wander among virus warriors helping the lonely

even the stones of families are weeping
in their opened graves with violent sorrow
for our future bones as we talk to shadows

with sincere blues we walk the plague wards
where there's no one to hear the lovely ones
dying no one left to bury the forgotten

that's why we shrink wrap ourselves in the liar's chair
and drag in grief's breath believing or not
we'll all meet again somewhere someday somehow

                                        --San Francisco

                        --Plum Village

Dreams Are Life
Oliver sopulu odo

I want to be like the things I dream, so I dream
Day & night, I become tomorrow's dreamer like a seer.
I dream today to see tomorrow, all my dreams
Are the reasons I can't sleep with my eyes close.

I understand that for you to make the world of your choice
You must dream like a winner who only knows
nothing but wins. I become a dreamer to
Become like tomorrow's gift.

I don't know tomorrow, though I dream to see
the things behind the things I dream.
I want to become my tomorrow's dreams, so I can become
that color I love seeing in my dreams.

I create tomorrow around me. I plant flowers today
and I dream the blooming, I dream the blossoming, and
the flowers grow like my tomorrow's dreams.
I end up learning how to hold dreams for tomorrow's victory.

See You In Hell
Jacob R. Moses

I'm not going where they condemn me
You're not going there either, friend

Wherever we go, I hope I see you

My breath would be an inferno
Lighting your path to a place
Within the heart of another

Aim for inspiration before expiration

For you are antidote and elixir
For you are potion and herbs

Everlasting manufactured damnation
Is not the place for you to ever go

Live to spite the hate mongers
Better than dying by their ignorance

Your ego is a non-negotiable melody
Belt out those bars and ignore
The terms of your endangerment

Be still in your convictions
Be active in your existence

Don't let kleptomaniacs steal your dignity
For you will write it out indecipherably
And keep it locked in a safe

Nobody will ever break it
Nobody can ever break you

THE ROT
Jonathan Watson

ahead of its arrival,
      people were still grappling
            with showing goodwill and
                 solidarity in the
age of these faceless and
      bottom-feeding factions
            with raging hatred, it
                 is clearly not beauty
that ensnares the senses,
      but rather truth that can
            be turned upside-down and
                 gutted before people

irrational enough to
      doctor photos and speak
            in a vacuum or rile
                 their base at a lectern,
banging their greedy fists and
      bottling the bitter succor
            for profit and quenching the thirst
                 of the so-called underdogs
deprived of the God-given
      right to slither upon people
            and spew their frosty venom
                 in a desperate grasp for heaven

a place that would not even
      accept them with their blood-stained
            hands partly filthy from their
                 index finger papercuts
picking out the words that bolster
      their notions but having no
            true sense of what they preach
                 and destroying people for it

they say these are the end times
        even though history has shown
                otherwise; we are just cannon
                        fodder to an amused maker

Seasonal Promise - An Etheree
Katrina Monroe

Bright
heads bob,
wave in the
sunny day's breeze.
Flowers extending
thanks for being planted
in the cold fall's muddy loam
so that this day might come, bringing
a message to all who persist in
the seasons of darkness, waiting on hope.

HAVE YOU BEEN BREATHING?
Katrina Monroe

Have you been breathing lately?
Really breathing?
By that I mean taking in from this world
the sustenance for your soul to survive?

Have you noticed the snowy egret down by the marina's edge?
Its poised stance, its alert eyes,
its beautiful white feathers, a royal robe shining in the sun,
while its feet parade in the water's muck.
It does not sully itself with the dirt of this world,
does not allow the earth's brownish substance
to cling to its pristine pinions.
It dedicates only the legs of its body to do the messy
and necessary work of wallowing to feed itself.
Meanwhile its calm demeanor signifies its belief
that all will be well eventually.

And have you watched the egret take off,
spreading wings so wide you could not imagine their size
when it was standing still?
High, higher…rising so fast in the air
that you are amazed at the strength of its slender body.
At times it joins its brethren,
other times suffers no rules, no limits
on its freedom to choose its singular destination.

And as it flies away from you,
have you felt some kinship,
learned some small lesson of importance,
noticed your breathing slow down?
Your mind calm, calmer…
And did your soul change?

I Saw The Light
Shirley Smothers

Someone asked me what my Near Death Experience was like.

For the first time since it happened more than 35 years ago I have found the courage to put it into written word.

When I was 29 years old I went into the hospital for a D and C (dilation and curettage). This procedure is common. Mine was being done because I had several Miscarriages within a short period of time.

I was placed under general anesthesia. During the procedure my tube ruptured. I, in fact had not had a miscarriage, but had a tubal pregnancy. My blood pressure went to nothing and my breathing was minimal. The doctors realized what was happening and were able to remove the ruptured tube. I was given a pint of blood and this saved my life.

But not before I had a NEAR DEATH EXPERIENCE. I was floating in the air. I looked down and saw myself lying on the operating table. My surgical team was all talking at once. I could not hear what they were saying, because there was a loud whooshing sound. But then there was nothing but blackness. What looked to be a million miles away was a faint light like a twinkling star. It grew bigger and stronger. It was vibrant and brilliant, but not blinding.

A voice said, "Shirley, time to go." I was like "What! No! I'm not dead!" The voice said, "Yes, it's time." I still refused to go. Other individuals who were refusing surrounded me. They all seemed to be unaware of the others. They were lost, desperate, desolate souls. We were between worlds. This world was nothing, just a bone chilling, bleak darkness. I saw people in the light. They seemed to be dancing and beckoning us. It seemed to be welcoming, loving and accepting. The Light seemed to say GOD IS THE LIGHT, AND THE LIGHT IS GOD. But yet, I refused.

Finally, the voice said, "You may return, there is a soul waiting to be born unto you." I returned, and then two years later, I had my son Matthew Smothers. So yes I was allowed to come back to give my Son a chance to be born. I also changed; I now know there is life after death. I have worked to make myself a better person and to help others to realize that they should work to make themselves better.

Reuters: "Some of the Partisans Were Women."
Vivien Cook

I will no longer be the woman in the doorway waving,
The shallow crumpled victim.
As easy to burn as crops or trees,
Or the dry gnarled tomb of houses.
Children attached as though by suction to the knees,
Arms outstretched to touch the bitter wind
That blows the fierce men westwards:
The soldiers, the marching ones.

The sun on my hair turns itself to the color of fire,
Or the faint swirl of marigolds
Left in some half-forgotten garden, but do not be misled.
I will no longer be the woman in the doorway waiting,
For the darting blur of renegades
Scrambling through the orchard.
Black birds thrown in handfuls at the sky,
Fear in my throat like needles.

Send my children far away into the dream country,
Give my children to old men
Who walk the fields
And know the names of flowers.
I am gone from the friendly clutter of this room
To some far horizon.
Board up the windows,
And let the soft creak of ants disturb the shadows.

I'll carve my name at crossroads
And spread a blanket where I sleep,
Desperate, unwavering.
Half awake and thinking clouds are men.
The ice-cold misery of killing
Is as close to me as doorways.
As close as the smudge
On the curve of the rind of the moon.

Look me squarely in the eye and understand.
I am ready to survive or die but with a gun in my hand.
I will no longer be the woman in the doorway waving

LONG DISTANCE HIKER: KODAK
Vivien Cook

Like tiny specks on the surface of the planet,
You belong to those who need to cover ground,
Half hypnotized by changing vistas.
Earth and rocks, the pathway sometimes indistinct
With every step the scenery changes.
Assessing variations of terrain and contour.
Sensitive to minor changes in the weather.
Shifts in barometric pressure, processed
As tactile shadows on skin and hair.
Strength of sun, wind direction, unpredictable..
Observant: the quickening of distant clouds
Harbinger of storms forming,
A sudden crack of thunder, getting nearer,
Thoughts of shelter just like any other animal.
Waiting for the end of lightning, hard flurry of hailstones.
Meeting others, dressed to survive.
The sporadic fleeting company of fellow hikers,
Greetings, gallery of stars, stories, leaving.
All with nicknames: Kodak, Gemini,
Yellow bear, White Eagle, Short Stack.
Alone again, time evaporates
Within the rhythm of the days blending,
You've come to occupy a private space
And understand yourself completely.
Somewhere between exhaustion and elation.
As close to happy as happy ever is.
One step at a time.
The chosen middle ground.
Contented.

Mycoepiphany
Tim Kahl

The bees began visiting a pile of rotting
wood chips, lifting them one by one
to get at the mycelium. They hovered
furiously as though driven by a higher
plan, an ideal transported from a seam
in the ether. The man who looked on
wondered whether they discovered it had
a deadly effect on viruses. Or did they
remember it? Perhaps it grew out of
a collective dream that swam east
out of the primordial depths..

Many years earlier the man had climbed
a tree in the middle of a storm and wailed
at the universe. It was the psilocybin talking,
but he was sure of his vision. His life would
be given over to fungus. He grew their networks
and turned them against toxic spills, turned
them into architecture. When the colonies
started to collapse, once again he returned
to the scene of the self-medicating bees.
But he couldn't rule out he invented it,
a growth in the thicket of neurons,
a hidden urge emerging from a dream.

History
Jeffrey Kingman

Young family out for a walk.
Mother's eyes distant, ruminating
baby in her arms has the same face
but eyes more intent on the present.
Father is accepting, holds little boy's hand
a boy who is silly, goofing as little boys do
and with his eyes crossed he looks
a little odd.
When the father tells us the boy is developmentally
delayed, we feel bad for not knowing what to say.
In 60 years, the historical record will report,
"In 2025, they were harmful to each other
because they didn't know any better."
In 60 years, there will still be war.
Like the one we're enduring right now, or worse.
They'll look back and think we didn't understand ourselves.
But we do know. We always know.

The Salvation of Love
Michael New

"The riches of Flora are lavishly strown."

Spring resurrects love's vigor.
May's sun thaws the hibernating
snake that stretches toward the warmth,
hungry for a furry mouse.

The grass on the hills flush with green,
the rosebuds exploding into red,
set the hearts of the two of us pulsing
with fiery blood, licked lips primed
for kissing, the tickling whisper in the ear,
the nibbling of a lobe in passing,
a reminder of the end in sight,
the throne of Eros, where we'll
press past our naked bodies in the bed
toward the future beyond winter's grave,
to the land of the imperishable ecstasy.

Coming from Church
Melody Anderson-Brumidis

You got to be cool,
which is the Golden Rule.
Be chill and
I will be there for you
no matter what you do.

Boys on green electric scooters
only go so fast.
Life's a song.
It doesn't last
only goes so long.

Second-story tour bus
on McAllister and Hyde.
Two girls hug in the middle of the street.
Skirts intersect.
Bright colors, so neat.

Israeli protests go another way.
War on Gaza Strip.
What a trip.
Bus driver uses our facilities.
Open door policy—you's and me's.

Farmers market
Sad furry fruit
passing hand-to-hand.
Money exchange is slow.
Fruits and vegetables
come and go.

Polk 19
Muni bus down the hill.
Out the way or
Your brains will spill.

Locals run uphill on Hyde.
Israel dancing
his happiness collides.

Smokers stack up
in front.
Everyone knows
Who's here
Who goes.
Girl in dress, lurch,
Sunday
Coming from church.

Shadows And Light
Daniel Miltz

In shadows deep where doubts reside
We feel the ache, we think with pride
A dance of light and dark within
Where certainty and questions spin
Through struggle's fire, our spirits soar
Emerging stronger, seeking more
Transitions whisper stories old
Epiphanies in hearts unfold
Transformations softly gleam
Like dawn upon a waking dream
Each challenge faced, a step anew
A journey through the shadow's hue
Certainty may flicker, fade
Yet hope persists, a guiding blade
In every stumble, every fall
New light is born—our soul's call

A Wider Light
Daniel Miltz

Perception shifts—the world tilts
What once was fixed now softly wilts
Each moment holds a different hue
And in the change, I find what's true
To hope, I hold with open hands
Like seeds I scatter in dry lands
Small acts of care—repair begun
A thread of light, a rising sun
I mourn the lost, but still believe
There's more to hold than just to grieve
Beyond the noise, I sense a thread
Of voices rising, not yet dead
I've learned that truth is often slow
And healing grows from what we show
Patterns form beneath the pain
A wider light, a deeper name

Battle Within
Connie Cyndi Chu

As one,
We are fighters,
Fighting a battle within us
Not with just mere weapons
But with our
hearts/minds/souls
We are self-determined
To seek love
In a world filled with hatred
To seek peace
In a world filled with chaos
To seek acceptance
In a world filled with intolerance
To seek hope
In a world filled with hopelessness
We can be warriors in and of our own right

Breaking Down the System
Connie Cyndi Chu

Blast all stereotypes and
all systematic injustices into smithereens
Slaying it so we can become a unifying force despite
our skin
our status
where we come from
we are one and the same-
we are all humans
we feel the same as others-
don't be a hater
be a lover
don't be shameful of who you are
be proud of what you have become

Interrupted Hands
Dianna Henning

> *Take from my hands some sun and some honey.*
> -Osip Mandelshtam

Osip Mandelshtam wrote poems
on the back of a dark horse.
What he said was a saddle.
Genius and its black eye
cantered by his side.
Natasha blew warm weather
onto his solitary fingers.
Both she and Anna conspired
to keep his work from banishment.
Late, late is my century,
Osip said to his bluing hands in transit.
Horses carried the prisoners
into Siberia's freezing cold.
Bruises and bedsores tagged Osip.
Bridled belief became honey,
and in the end even the cloud-riddled sky
blew doves over his birthplace.

Tangerine
Brandon Vu

I peeled it because
It has to be   perfect.

         good or bad day
you used to come upstairs
And hand me a bowl of
          fruit.

The   glow
from the tangerine

always caught
          my attention. I savor

                  each one and it reminds me of
          how you'd pick   apples from
                  the same bowl

because you knew I liked
          tangerines   the most.

fingertips   orange
                  from peeling.
                          I imagine you
you bringing a bowl to my future
children. Someday
          I know they would pick
your favorite.

The provenance of serendipity
Anne M Carson

In a somewhat serene state of mind
you go dip dip dipping into the world
throwing lines of curiosity into well, web, welter

Whenever I dip for it Horace Walpole wrote in 1754
describing his newly minted *serendipity* to a friend
Accidental sagacity is how he put it, wanting to emphasise

the skill of sniffing things out   He didn't hold with
serendipity just befalling someone like the jolt of a missed step
To him it was as individual as a quirk, a gesture, a gait

Drawing on the etymology of sagacity, its olfactory implications
he highlighted the nose's capacity for discernment
NO discovery of a thing you ARE looking for he quips

comes under this description   Serendipity, the word falls
undulant from the tongue   Happy-sounding word for a beneficial
happening you have had some hand in

Phantom in the Tantrum
Amana Mission

It's half past when what should have been
Silly jackrabbit's running late
As a quintessential tribunal convened
To irony out my fate
Ye stand accused of high treason
And torturing poor reason
Yes, charged with killing time
It's bend the knee or sail the sea
And walk the plank without a rhyme

Swinging from a Gordian knot
Withered by glares of thousand mile stares
Twin imposters bound and gagged on the altar
Banished forever from both hide and hair
Sentinel waves rising and sinking
The clouds are grooving and the moon is winking
The fortunes are legion and plots are Cartesian
Arguing with oracles was none too wise
Falling through cracks and untold seasons
But like Socrates, I ain't here to apologize

So now it's Dublin or nothing
Those Heros, zeros, and Neros
Egos roasted at the stake
The story is left to the dreamer who knows
It's persist or perish at the whim of the wake
Darkness spans horizons and large winds blow
Luck is easier to break than to make
The wild tides fall as fast they rose
Escaping with a splatter and a shake

Spirits in a decanter
A message in a flask
Flickering shadows answer
What the lens of senses ask

With all these splintered eyes to see
In the night lies dawn's stark destiny

There's a ghost in the host
As ready as I'll never be
Yearning and returning to hopes of being free
There was a genie in that bottle
And that bottle, it was me

E=MCC unlocked by the swerving of Mercury
Fabricating space-time through gravity

Synthesizing thought-bombs in the laboratory
Tell me one thing you know to be so
Get tossed by the current or become the flow
And how do you know what you don't know?
Tell me tales of blood and bone
Conveyed in subtle variations of tone
How do you know what you don't know?
It's there in relief like the carving in stone

On which side of history are we now?
Port or starboard, or by and by the bow?
One blink past the last place you'd look
On the first page of an open and dusty book
The wish itself is enchanted
Taken for and being granted
Like a tease trying to keep those options open
But the essence of genius demands devotion

A phantom haunts the tantrum
Moaning and groaning in psychic chains
Rudely insecure and insufferably vain
A why which applies to long forsaken pain
And who is this you? Who is this I?

Is it more than the sum of covert motivations
Unburied by diamond mining excavations
Revealed to be nothing more than reaction formations

An interface of inner and outer space
It's a place to hang your hat on
Look, if we're we're being real about it
Who I am is none of my business
I is a lie, does it even exist?
And yet my head must have somewhere to sit

Spirits in a decanter
A message in a flask
Flickering shadows answer
What the lens of senses ask
With all these splintered eyes to see
In the night lies dawn's stark destiny
There's a ghost in the host
As ready as I'll never be
Yearning and returning to hopes of being free
There was a genie in that bottle
And that bottle, it was me

Soiree of Stars
Dr. Shilpa Chakravarty

The evening sky, that's pale orange,
Bids adieu to the day;
Plunging into the night's bliss
It wipes off the lines of stress away.

Enough has each one worked, since morning,
Much trouble you've tried to solve.
Now is the time to get along with loved ones,
The peace around them does revolve.

The diurnal beasts and birds return home,
The nocturnal creatures will now, prey, eat and sleep.
The time it is, to slip yourself into slumber,
Do not disturb the night's dark cover.
Let the stars be with the moon,
For their soiree shall end soon;
The dawn's vermillion hue is about to peep.

The rays of dawn flash
Upon the multitude of creatures on earth,
Waking them to adore
The enchanting beauty of hers.

Money, Adventure, and Danger
Hilary King

A coyote cries the night
we get a call from the bank.
They're everywhere,
my husband and I agree.

We scramble to find our cats,
a kitten named Adventure,
a calico, Danger, down
to his last three teeth.

Somebody tried to use
our credit card
in a hamburger joint
Hamburgler, my husband says.

The coyote cries again,
short and piercing.
We stare through screens
at the darkness.

Adventure hides under the bed.
Danger sits by the door.
Does he hear it the fourth time
the coyote cries?

We cancel the long string of numbers
that meant so much to us.
Our next cat I'll let run free,
call its name from the door:
Guilty! Guilty! Guilty!

Never Been Up This High Before
Cassandra M. Walton

Never been up this high before
Been in the lower lines at the bowels and cesspools of life
On barricaded streets with roadblocks
Cardboard beds (made of boxes) line my block

Loud sirens of ambulances, screeching police cars, and fire alarms
Guns drawn on those unarmed
Discarded lives standing around burning trash cans to keep warm
This is the picture that serves daily as my backdrop
Yeah, that's the view on my block

Never been quite this high before
Next door neighbors are a figment of my imagination
More like next to the "ground & floor" neighbors

Although surrounded by a city of towering buildings and spectacular
lights
Houses on monstrous mountains and hill tops
My staircase always seems to be in a downward direction

Always seem to find my way at the bottom of things
Like my housing—my food found in the lower parts of
the garbage and trash cans
I said I've never been up this high before

Basements—no light at the end of my tunnel—no window to see
through
Holding my hands out, as I also try using them to pull myself up

Perhaps my burdens and bags are just a little too heavy
to be lifted out of this situation
As I am pushing my way through life with possessions in a shopping
cart
Trying to do the very best I can
With empty bottles

and soda cans
Brown paper bags full of nothing
Watching as people and good fortune always seem to be passing me
by
Ocean and waterfront views
Green trees and the smell of rose gardens
May line your streets

Abandoned buildings, cars, and forgotten and abandoned lives line
my street
Alley cats and straggling dogs become my enemy
Fighting for the crumbs that drop from the master's table
And the only waterfalls that I really see from this view are my tear
drops
That have formed a river that flows with no end in sight

Perhaps I feel if I weep just a little longer I will cause my
own tsunami
I'd pray for death if I thought I could be buried above ground
Never been quite this high before
And although today I stand wearing torn and tattered clothing
In borrowed heels only two inches high
And two steps above things
I've never been up this high before

People of the world
Dina Oraz

There are people who, like the sun, give energy to the world,
With radiance and warmth they warm everything around them.
There are people like stars, who shine brightly,
They shine bright, they're not hot.

There are people like the moon, dreaming of something,
What's on their minds, who knows?
There are people from Venus, they're fantastic,
They're incomprehensible, even fabulous.

There are those who must be from the fearsome Mars,
They howl with everybody, they do not know the farce.
There are Saturn men and Pluto men,
They'll never take their crowns off in front of you.

There are Jupiter men who will crush you to a pulp,
And they'll trip you up easily.
There are Mercury men who are an enigma to the system,
They're fast, they're silent, they use schemes.

There are the Uranians, they give off radiation,
Dangerous influence, contamination.
There are the Neptune people, cold to all,
Their hearts chained with eternal ice.

There are Earth people, of perfect light,
They understand you without word or answer,
A look is enough, no hint is needed.
There are men of the earth who can't be angry or reproachful.

There are men who are like snow, sobering the brain,
They will never melt before you.
There are men like the wind, they are changeable.
What's in their heads? I don't know, they're stubborn.

There are people like rain, they suffer and cry,
They don't hide their feelings under a mask.
There are people who burn like fire,
They control the fate of others with ease.

There are people of water, oceans, elements,
They proudly present themselves as a mission.
There are people like air - airy, empty,
So far from the world, from reality.

There are people who are volcanoes, spewing gas,
They don't help, they burn, they shout.
And those who are on their backs, they make them sweat,
They're people who are swamps.

There are people Fogs - hurts, wounds.
There are people Stop cranes, such chumps.
There are people Sands, they swallow them up,
They open up helplessness, fear inside.

Some people are like avalanches, sweeping everything away,
They can't breathe and won't let go.
There are people who are comets and meteors,
We all look up to them.

There are people who are magnets and people who are titans,
They protect us all like talismans.
There are people who are dawns and people who are sunsets.
Wise and educated aristocrats.

There are people of galaxies and people of orbits,
Friendly, kind and open to all.
There are people of the universe who are immense,
Strong, independent, honest, tolerant.

There are people like humans - they don't throw away a word,
They always help others in any way they can.
And there are people of peace on this planet,
I wish there were more of them in the world!

No matter how many people are wandering around,
It's important to keep the light of the soul in the darkness!

After the Election
Gail Newman

We spoke of what mattered-- family, friends.
We spoke of silence, how if you stand still in the forest
the trees seem to speak.
Just then the wind rose and shook the sycamores,
a pair that towered above us
forming a canopy, *an umbrella*, Judy observed.
Yellow leaves fell on the redwood deck and in our hair.
We laughed then for no reason.
A grandchild had been born.
A wedding, a separation.
Gone to heaven the caregiver reported over the phone.
Died, Debra said.
We were not afraid of words
or truth.
We had never known war, not from close up.
We had been spared so much.
Still the world was hurt, splintered and broken.
The news entered the conversation
like a wound we could not heal
or understand.
It was enough for these hours
to sit together, to eat salad and cake,
to drink coffee and talk of the past.
It was enough to be together
for a few small hours
and let the future lie down like a tired dog
asleep under the table.

I Bring Myself to the Garden
Amanda Fall

I bring myself to the garden
aching with exhaustion, bleary-eyed
after yet another sleepless night.
I wrap myself in paint-peeling sweatshirt
and plaid pajamas, stuff my feet
in rain boots, grateful for trees on all sides,
the freedom to be with no eyes on me except my son,
the dog, the cat; maybe chestnut-backed chickadees,
and ever-present slugs and snails.

I carry my woes to the garden,
my body a worn-out suitcase
heavy with what was. And when I say garden,
of course I really mean the patch of dirt
and scrub grass I am determined to transform
into a butterfly-fluttering, bee-buzzing sanctuary
of zinnia and hollyhock and poppy.
I bought a dusty box of cheap seeds, too,
claiming to contain coneflower and coreopsis,
a cottage-grove fantasy made real.

And by reality, of course I mean
a dirt-under-my-fingernails kind of truth,
a scrabbling-my-way-back from dark of night
and whisper of despair only 3 a.m. can hold.
Of course I mean I, too, am a dirt patch
waiting to bloom, a neglected weedy bit of land
coming back to life, one blister and
handful of hope at a time.

Blue Light Seems

Cleo Griffith

Blue light seems benign
like the Blue Fairy or icebergs,
but it has deceived me,
now I am sleepless,
all hours seem like daylight,
I find I must give up
evening sessions on
tablet, phone, computer,
because in my sleepless state
I am a stumblebum knocking about.
I need to sleep, not sleepy,
but I need to sleep, to wrench myself
away from solitaire, scrabble,
my lonely pursuit of aimless winnings.
I am one of the victims
of the world's blue-light madness,
tricked by innocuous glow
into a 24-hour daylight,
I must turn off each machine,
take a stack of books, read myself
to sleep, if I can find that
secret place again.

When All is Lost
Evie Groch

With its gnarled growth
of twisted branches,
the blackened oak tree
stands in stoic silence,
contemplating the dire
devastation in which its
devoted roots keep it.

Little hope of restoration,
its trunk erodes as easily
as the ruins of destroyed
cities that surround it.

The ravages of war, fire,
floods, famines contaminate
what's left of life, erasing
the scents of the season,
the logic of reason.

And then, when all is lost,
a fresh green leaf appears
on a lifeless limb of the forsaken
oak, awakening it to dream
of renewed life, as renewed
as a babe found in the ruinous
rubble of a broken city,
brought up to breathe again
in an unexpected unveiling
of resilience and rejoicing.

The Rationing of Empathy

Evie Groch

In such short supply, dwindling still,
this commodity, free to produce, free to
distribute, is a rare one.

One only has to decide to be mindful of it,
let it flow to irrigate the landscape,
reap gratitude.

A doctor soothing a mother in delivery,
a teacher overflowing with patience engaging
her low-ability students in meaningful learning,
a critic offering a poet feedback with compassion,
a rejection letter composed as an invitation to resubmit.

A volunteer encouraging a student learning to read,
a librarian setting aside a pile of books on trains
for the second grader who always asks for some,
a barista who squeezes an extra pump of chocolate
into a café mocha for a chocoholic,
a motorist who stops for the grandma and her
granddaughter in the crosswalk,
the produce man who cuts an orange open
for you to taste before you commit.

If we all practiced it, there would be
more than enough to go around.
Let's build up our reserve daily so we
can accompany one another through
life's contrary contractions.

Whisper of Doubts

Maribel Passion

The road was rough, the nights were long,
I stumbled through, where I didn't belong,
Whispers of doubt, a shadow blind,
But I held the fire deep in my mind.

Every step a fight, every breath a plea,
The weight of the world pressing on me,
Yet in the cracks, where light would stream,
I built a bridge from broken dreams.

I rise, I shine through the stormy air,
Turning pain into stripping despair,
With doubts behind and certainty near,
I've found my voice; I've found my cheer.

The mirror cracked but the truth was clear,
In my reflection strength appeared,
I've danced with chaos, I've fought my pain,
Through the ashes, I rise again.

The stars once seemed so far to touch,
Now they're close, I feel them now,
The doubts have melted, certainty glows,
I've become the story, only I could compose.

July 2025
Elizabeth Greene

> Evil was active in the land. . . .
>   --H.D.
> We are living in a time of monsters.
>   --Charlie Angus

My birth shadowed by the horror of the last war,
I'd hoped uneasy peace would last my life,
never expected my old age would be a time of monsters,
never thought the country I was born in
would be overrun by lies, black, sticky as tar.
Never thought I'd see groups of five or six masked thugs,
ICE on their backs, surround workers in fields,
walkers on streets, parents, grandparents,
disappear them to private jails or Alligator Alcatraz,
deport them to El Salvador or the Sudan.
What's the bounty for each body?

Due process?
Was there due process in the Holocaust?
Or Stalin's Russia?
I never thought it would happen here—
good and evil turned inside out.
Criminals pardoned, the innocent detained.

What do you do in a time of monsters?
Wish for a hero with a magic wand or sword?
Or cling to truth, to words diamond hard,
call things by the names,
kidnapping, corruption,
hang onto everyone you love,
connect to the mycelium resistance network,
search for the "true rune, the right spell"
to help transform the age.

Black
Walid Abdallah

I have always been called black
Before my eyes and behind my back

I always try to hide my sufferings and tears
I have to stand more than anyone bears

I didn't create myself nor my color
That becomes my weakness and their power

I may be black from the outside
But I have the whitest heart inside

My color has become the curse of my own race
On earth, we no longer have a place

I am cursed in every place I go
I always feel so little and low

I was born only to suffer
My feeling does not matter

For any crime, I am the first to blame
The Nigro did it and call my name

My soul is imprisoned within the dark skin
My own color has become my own sin

I hope people will see the beauty in my heart
And stop excluding me and asking me to depart

My heart breaks a thousand times every day
Nobody cares about me, no attention they pay

I am a caged bird left lonely in a rainy night
With broken wings, with no power to fight

Outcast and cursed that is how I feel
In front of their vanity I must kneel

I hope they will understand we complete each other
We were created to reconstruct the earth together

We have the same soul but different colors
We have charming scent from various flowers

I dream of a world in which we are all the same
And only a human being becomes our name

We should teach our children the power of tolerance
And root out every envy, hatred and intolerance

I love and respect everyone on this earth
I have been taught this since my birth

Mint Tea
Walid Abdallah

Upon my hand, the mint tea spilled and burned,
In flames and pain, my love to ash was turned.
I watched the scar, the rising smoke and flame,
And wondered why such harm from love became.

How fiercely can the things we cherish sting—
This bitter truth that hurtful moments bring.
That day, I mourned a sorrow deep and wide:
The tea I loved held no love to confide.

Folded Wings
Murray Eiland

A swirl of color floats upon the sky,
Born from the nectar of blooms fresh and bright,
Each petal's sweetness calls these creatures forth,
Their fragile dance—a fleeting glimpse of life.
In months, a cycle spun, then tragedy,
As some are caught by fate or folly's grip—
In webs of silk or talons sharp and keen,
Yet still, resilient, others brave the chill,
Through icy nights where hunger gnaws their wings.

Above the fields they soar on painted sails,
No shelter found, just sunlight's warm embrace,
As storms release their torrents, fierce and wild,
These gentle beings weather every change.
To think the lore of ages spun their tales—
Of butter, milk—of witches' whispered craft,
As if they stole earth's gifts with unseen hands,
Yet truth unfolds: they seek the humble weeds,
The common ground where life begins anew.

O gardeners, with hands intent to tame,
Beware the zeal that ruins nature's way,
For in the chase to make a perfect space,
You lay to waste the feast that butterflies
Hold sacred, their abundance swept away.
These winged delights, with colors bold and bright,
Stand witness to the balance that we break.
In innocence, they flit from bloom to bloom,
Their beauty once thought cursed, yet truly grace.

Squickly couldn't understand
Krzysztof T. Dabrowski

Squicky couldn't understand the world's cruelty.

He once saw something called the Muppets in a big rectangle through an opening in the human seat. Piggy Pig was one of the Muppets, and he couldn't take his eyes off her.

He dreamt he would also succeed and become a piganizer and appear in all the Muppet's houses to win her heart.

Years passed, and nothing came of these dreams. Not only was he still stuck in the hovel, but there were rumors he would be the next to be eaten by people. Chrumk and Pinky, with their families, had already disappeared.

Hey Baudelaire
Virginia Barrett

Your poem described how sailors
recklessly-long at sea, made greedy

for diversion would capture an albatross
just to watch it flounder on the ship,

ridiculing its attempts to navigate
the deck, clumsy and shamed pulled

from the air, its great wings dragging
like oars at its sides, no longer in

its element, majestic in the sky and
able to haunt the tempest soaring

on storm winds . . . as we the People,
captured in these times and bullied

by brutes, are hindered from walking
with grace.

Laundry Day—Socks
Virginia Barrett

I do my laundry at the Olema campground. After the storms
it's flooded, a little lake we might swim in were it summer
and conditions different. We slept here once, it was damp
ground then too, but not enough to complain—watery
dreams beside the creek where coho swim to spawn.

I'm the only one here except for the woman in the
backroom who tends the place and smells of cigarettes. She
helped me when I didn't notice a Canadian quarter had
slipped into my stash and the dryer wouldn't work. An
image of the Queen, dead now after so much time.

A young guy comes in with a load and fills the machine I
just used. Almost done with my chore, I'm tired of reading
poems downloaded on my phone from the library. Soon I
find myself watching his machine once he goes outside to
the parking lot to lean into the back of his truck, apparently
sorting things out.

In the round window of the front-loading machine a sock
Catches my eye as it briefly rotates by. It's my sock (did I
forget to take it out?)—but no, it's just *like* my sock,
probably ordered from the same ubiquitous online shop we
should all boycott if we weren't lazy and the pandemic
hadn't thrust us into even more indolence by keeping us in
lockdown for so long.

A woman's multicolored sock, part wool, it comes in a
variety pack of five (I gave one pair to my niece for
Christmas so now I have four). Evidently this young man
has a girlfriend, or a wife? Maybe they're his mother's. I
think of all our intimate articles: how at any given moment
somewhere we may have the same of something on as the
next person in line, say like in the supermarket. The great
global market; we're all becoming carbon-copy consumers.

Robin Williams (rest his comic soul) wore rainbow-colored
Socks on a talk show I saw once. Given the way trousers
rise, sitting in the chair made them prominent—quirky and
Mork-like—totally him, though I bet someone, somewhere
in the world had on those exact same socks that day, unless
they were one-of-a-kind like Neruda's, handknit by Maru
Mori and celebrated in an ode.

The sun is setting and the clouds glow orange-red. The
dryer's heat is not what it could be. I feed it more quarters
while the earth slowly absorbs the rain and the trees feel the
ghosts of the limbs they've lost in these weeks of stormy
winds. You, who camped here with me once, gone now too.
May all our feet be warm.

Why We Are Here
Marilyn LoRusso

We are here
To watch flowers unfold
and play with the wind
To watch the sun rise and set
and feel the blue of the sky

We are here
To laugh as lizards do pushups
and listen to birds sing, really listen

We are here
To run to the top of a hill and twirl
and drink from a mountain stream
To blow a tune on a blade of grass
and count petals on daisies

We are here
To feel the smoothness of a rock
and the roughness of tree bark
We are here

To listen to the sea in a conch
and gather crispy leaves for jumping
To lay in a field of tall grass
and count the animals in clouds

We are here
To whisper in an infant's ear,
"You can BE anything"

Children Tasting Doom
Clare Olivares

When the sirens screeched
we ducked under our desks
if it was recess
we flattened ourselves on the playground
in rectangular formation
a perfect target
Mister Khrushchev wanted us dead
and not even the President could stop him
After the siren's wail stopped
our teachers told us to run home
never knowing what was test and what was real
the faster I ran the safer I felt
"Close all the windows and doors, hide in a confined space"
the narrow hallway a sanctuary from fallout
nuclear fallout, a phrase everyone dreaded
I thought it would fall from the sky like snow
once touched BOOM! instantly vaporized
Mother said fallout was invisible
believed we could see it with special glasses
but we had none
unseen snow that kills on contact
no safe place to hide
children lived tasting doom
waiting and watching for flashes in the sky
imagining the neighbor's sunflowers withering
and Rex the dog next door who could jump a six foot fence
would not be able to jump high enough

Untitled in Blue
Gabriella Garofalo

To P.

Why do you keep the clouds?
Trash them out, darkness has an expiry date,
And Spring got it wrong, no flowers, no clouds,
Hardly a shivering blue, night and her heaps
Of scattered stars, when sham seasons loom over souls,
Words, skies, and survival comes in handy-
Same old story, you know, but what's that,
No free food for souls, just those tenants
Of the underwood, clouds in God's eyes,
Waves, and a different life if she wheezes
Among slant words, so very young, so naive
When mixing up stars and shadows,
Or leaping in fear into seasons, and trees-
And ambos, alarms, lost bits all left in the dark,
No need for maps or rhumbs, just snatch her up,
Yes, light, and you, moon, don't screw around,
Leave them alone, rooms, streets, hidden places,
Play the game if she says blue will see to it,
Giving you shelter if you freeze from the cold-
Drop dead, shadows, on the border of her soul,
As the briars of her blue are growing,
And no, the skies won't fall down
Among scantily-clad girls, half-naked men
Wrestling in the heat,
Or songs she rescued from water-
See? Just like Moses.

To S.

Been hanging around for long, sky?
The days are gathering to bring back the soul
To the grass you snatched her from,
The smokeless blue flame is coming,
The partner to your greedy hands,
Your reason as fruits rot,
A cheap light is spreading
Her percussive blue all over the house-
But no need for high drama, soul,
Don't go ablaze when breath blows you,
Or hope looking for shelters
Shifts your crippled limbs:
Same old stuff never ends, maybe loss,
Maybe desert, old bags lying still as light,
As their wounded, scraped voice
Orders the shadows, and dries up
The echo in your eyes-
Careful now, soul, the sky looks stark,
Just a handful of slag as you stumble
On stubborn births, dispersing clouds,
And high tension writes the electric blue
On the dark that burns your fingers-
But don't kid yourself, just hide
Your thirst among hushed memories, broken limbs,
Poetry, prayers, who cares about names,
As long as they play along with water, or daffs,
Just look for your erewhon, right,
Even a bloody trench of rattling bodies
While cops are yanking away
Two young black tramps who might taint-
Heaven forbid-
The pure white of a lovely station.

I will not be shaken

Abigail Brown

I will not be shakin' nor will I be shook by another halfway crook who ran off with my heart right from the very start I knew this wouldn't be smart I feel like I'm drifting away slowly falling apart I will not be shaken nor will shook I'll think of my next words to go into that hook open up to the important page in this biography of a book don't let the phrase I speak be mistaken or mistook I'll never be shaken scared because I cannot be shaken and nor shall I be shook because I'm the empress of my book I will not be shaken.

anamnesis
Emma A.Woodard

It was growing pains, they said.
Recess drama. The ache of new schools.
Just puberty. You're thirteen.
It was homework. Stress. Nerves.
The looming specter of SATs.

It was the fourth thin envelope of rejection,
the lost title of Valedictorian,
the weight of a cap and gown.
It was female issues, your weight,
your attitude, your whirling hormones!
It's your period.

A side effect of the medication,
or perhaps not serious at all.
Are you sure it's not just mental?
With a history like yours,
it's all in your head.
Your doctors are lying.

Have you tried hiking? More weed? Less weed?
A better balance? It's not that hard.
Everyone else is surviving.
Your grandfather with his prostate of bone
did not complain like this.
You are so much weaker. Are you sure
you're even related?

It's genetics. It's in your head.
There won't be anything wrong.

There's never anything really wrong.
Until it was.
A lump. A hard, silent fact.

Why didn't you say?
We could have helped.

Were you neglecting your body?
Your husband must not touch you often.
How often do you have sex?

You're not married? But you…

It became the weight of promiscuity,

the color of your lipstick,
the shade of your dyed hair,
a fault-line for your insecurities.
Your fault, that miscarriage.
Your fault, for sleeping with queers.
We tried to save you from yourself.

You were an angry child,
a terrible teen, you see things
that aren't there. Look what you've done
to your mother's nerves.

It was because you were bad.
We were good.
You got yourself into this mess.
You should have had better insurance.

A better job. You can't take time for chemo.
Are you dying? We can't have you
working here like this.
You were not dedicated. You were difficult.

You will stop soon.
It will be quiet again.

You will be good again.
Was it just in my head?
Doctor, it was right under your nose.

Alone in San Francisco
Lalit Kumar

Sauntering down the Embarcadero
Along the edges of pier 39,
A foggy morning clings to the city,
Rumbling itself awake from slumber.

I trudge along the wooden pier,
The waves lap at the jetty
The winds howl in my ears
A pelican nonchalantly flaps its wings
And flies past my view ahead.

It's not so lonely, after all
The nature is resplendent in its spread today,
The winds, the waves, the ocean
Seem to have no bearing
To the seasons of my mind.
Nature is constant,
My mind shifts with each seed of thought.

I am not so lonely, after all
I open my arms
To welcome the oncoming wind
feeling it directly on my face.
I let it caress
My skin and my face
I feel it ruffle my hair,
And I close my eyes to
Witness the love of my friend.

I jump in the oncoming waves
The blues of Pacific
Is as cold, as the thaw in my heart.
It's an instant commingling
Of two long lost lovers

For whom the distance has not dimmed
The light of their hearts.

Distant memory has a way of its own
To ebb and flow with the tide.
A dream can rise aflutter with the waves
Or sink to the bottom
With the changing tides, and time.

The ocean water
I feared it may drown me,
Instead it taught me,
how to swim with the tide.

The Joshua Tree of Mojave

Lalit Kumar

Dry, arid, desert landscape of Mojave
spartan-like, feisty under the relentless sun,
austere rock outcrops, shrubs,
wildflowers under the clear blue sky,
bloom vividly upon a thousand stars in the cover of the night.
A solid trunk of a tree, a poetry
unfurls its branches in a twisted scape
gazing straight upon the starry night,
in deep contemplation of its sparse existence.
Eking out a living of its own,
resilient,
the root seeks water through the fault lines of the desert.
Standing alone in sublime beauty of its harsh climes,
radiating joy to the lone hiker.
In the beauty of a silhouette, it emerges
the Joshua tree of Mojave.

Cloud gazing translates into other forms too
Zach Beach

I've always seen things in other things:
the magnolia bursting from crashing sea foam,

rivers running through cobblestone,
exploding starfish in orange lilies,

knots of trees keeping their eyes on me,
ancestors dancing in the fire,

dreams fading in the smoke.
There are faces falling with the rain—

marcona almonds in each drop.
This morning

we made moon pancakes,
painted our water with tea,

curled the bed sheets like parsley.
Your mouth
a widening cave inviting

me to explore.
The mystery of love

is seeing what no one else sees.
Tell me

honeyheart,
what do you see?

La Limpieza
Maiah A. Merino

dressed in White I arrive
prepared for a time
              we sit in no time

              donde, el humo sagrado nos limpia—where, the
sacred smoke cleans us

awake to the Altar of living
aware of reciprocity divining
nuestros alimentos son nuestras medicinas: our foods are our
medicines
                                  maíz
                                      platanos
                                            chocolate
                                                pimientos
                                                      chiles
                                                              rosas

invitamos a los elementos
esperamos a los visitantes—susurramos a nuestros antepasados
we invite the elements
await the visitors—whisper to our ancestors

                                  no blood is shed here
                                  Our souls feasted.

*Published by the Redmond Poet Laureate, Ching-In Chen's 2025,
"Read Local Eat Local" poetry postcard project, Redmond, WA*

Two Books (a duplex)
Maiah A. Merino

I inherited two books when I left for school
he left school in 6th grade and became a man.

    A 6th grader was left to buy food again:
    you don't have to be good to be left.

I've been good my whole life, except
I've been unable to digest the incest.

    It takes worms a while to digest the compost,
    carrier of their sins, soiled as their host.

Drawn to prisms, light carriers transform again.
I baptized my doll, releasing her of seeded sin.

    Sometimes baptismal waters accelerate new worth.
    Sometimes the gold we carry is transferred in words.

The gold we share is the dust between us.
I inherited two books when I left for school.

The Headline Was Wrong
Angelica Blyden

They said the city was dying.
But I tasted lumpia, passed hand to hand
'cross backyard tables.
Tamales wrapped in foil,
poke stretched 'cross platters,
pozole simmering beside collard greens.!

They said the city was dying.
But I saw a bubblegum pink quinceañera dress on Broadway.

Scrapers grind through alleyways,
refusing to stay silent.
Each bassline shakes the block,
rattles the windows,
pounds against my chest.

We bend but do not break.
Our rhythm is stubborn,
our pulse is too loud for silence.

Children cover walls
with rivers and rainbows,
painting over wounds,
proving beauty can rise
from what was left behind.

Every pothole we step over,
every eviction we survive,
every time the lights flicker
we remain.

The headline was wrong.
We are not dying.
We are the roots cracking concrete,
the flame that refuses to burn out.

Repair
Angelica Blyden

Some things break loud.

Some things break quiet.

A marriage.

A levee.

A window in riot.

I thought repair was glue
it's not.

It's hands.

Steady.

True.

Hands that hold the fragments slow,
gentle enough to let healing grow.

We speak into fractures
like sutures,
like prayer.

Soft words binding
what broke there.

Not perfect,
not whole,
but closer than before.

Repair is the courage
to open the door.

At the Open Wound of the World
Elizabeth Kirkpatrick-Vrenios

is Narcissus, night after night,
staring into a cesspool
at the distorted image of media as Echo,
Truth lies at the bottom
beyond reach.

Weather startles the earth open like an egg,
rivers snarl with that sssssh
repeating night after night
a promise of never.

Grass, stiff and brown,
candy wrappers in its teeth,
daggers our dancing.
We uproot forests,
redwoods whimper as they topple,
we replace birdsong with insistent
whines & thrums of chainsaws.

Our Mouths savor the xenophobic tang
of slaughter. We ape anthems,
night after night that throb
with hungry songs, insistent,
well-dressed,
untouchable.

We wield bombs as easily as
we unfold umbrellas,
& puncture the land
with hypodermics
for blood, black & pooled
to power our Hummers.

Mega shelves are stuffed
with chips & soda, stickered vegetables

shrouded in plastic.
Corpulent Narcissist with Echo attached
to his ear, succumbs to corporations
that hawk sugary colas,
twinkies, potato chips, TV dinners,
Bibles, sweatpants, American cheese.

Truth, no longer a spotted leopard,
now sports the dark gloss of panther
 & night after night stalks
a miracle that never comes.

The Accidental Bouncer
Matt J. McGee

Reilly is in San Francisco for 24 hours
so he texts Heather to meet him out front
of Lefty O'Douls on Geary. He arrived first
so he stood statuesque beside the door,
arms folded over the new black t-shirt
covering his hockey player's chest.
He tucked his long red beard into his shirt
and waited.

Half a minute later
two of Frisco's chattiest
gym-toned vegetarians approached
and perfunctorily handed over their IDs.
Reilly accepted, and seeing that their simultaneous
text and talk wasn't going to stop,
he waved them in with a nod.
By the time Heather showed up
Reilly had checked seven people
and was sitting beside his first beer,
on the house.

"In town for two hours
and you've already got a job."
She opened her wallet and handed over her license.
He wanted to say something funny, ironic,
but after a quick glance he said:
"this is expired."

She took it back. Sure enough.

"I can't let you in.
What if my boss finds out?"

She leaned into him,
set her palm against the chest

that slapshots had built and whispered
the naughtiest thing she knew.

The breeze rising off the bay
swayed his beard, and he muttered:
"Lucky for you, this is
my last day on the job."

Alternative Transport
Matt J. McGee

If you're not the flying type
and don't feel up to a five hour drive,
there's only one other way to the Bay Area
from my oak-laden town, and it's pretty disappointing.
You'd think trains would roll into Frisco day and night,
at least into Oakland anyway, but no; trains only reach
Santa Maria from here, our halfway point, and then
it's a long slow George & Lenny ride through Salinas
until somewhere in the late evening, fog reveals
Fisherman's Wharf and off you all go, thinking
how much easier it'd be to find a good meal
if it wasn't for all these damn tourists.

How to Stay Afloat
Shawna L. Swetech

Some days you feel like a passenger
on the Titanic, the one playing piano
to calm everyone's nerves as the ship
slips into those dark depths. But today,
you see a video clip of a young man
in a yellow safety vest, sharing water
with a thirsty squirrel, as it splays
across a hot sidewalk. The man tipping
his own plastic bottle right into
the small open mouth. Tears well,
as you watch the man gently pet
the squirrel's back with his free hand,
the squirrel's front leg outstretched,
its tiny paw resting on the man's other hand.
You watch it run up the man's forearm
and stay there, the man still pouring
water even though something wild
is standing on his arm, and his sleeve
is soaked. And you think, wow—
if everyone just cared this deeply.
If everyone shared water, kindness,
anything needed, maybe we could
keep this thing afloat. Maybe
we could stay.

For Sharon

Jennifer Sweeney

Together we rose,
Rose from the ashes of our pasts.
Not like the graceful bird,
But clawing and kicking until
We could breathe again.

Together we rose,
On our own paths
But always there-
Supporting, laughing, crying.
Just there, always there.

Until you weren't.

There was your call-
The fear, the hope for it to be anything else.
But no. Diagnosis to death- 10 months.

And together now we rise again,
Keeping your memory alive
Through laughter and tears.
A year and a day since you left this world.
Our beautiful bestie.

June 18, 2025

Silence
Jennifer Sweeney

The silence
Before the sunlight cracks the horizon,
Before the new day begins.
Lying in bed watching the
Dull light push back the darkness,
My dog's head heavy on my legs.
The silence is comforting,
The silence is safety.

Snap
Martha Ellen Johnson

1. Stormy morning. At dawn
I arrive at the Senior Center
for a morning meeting. The
homeless are already awake,
gathered around a small light
outside blue plastic tarps tethered
to the old railing across the street
near the demolished Safeway.
Men with scruffy beards. Thin
women in filthy clothes. Sometimes
a companion dog or kitten.
Shopping carts stuffed with junk.
A man eyes the donation of
produce outside the Center.
"For Members Only"
He reaches for an apple. Our
eyes meet. Will I snitch?
"Be sure and take enough
for later," I tell him. Susan
scolds me. "That's for us.
They can have what's left a 4."

A woman in a broken-down
wheelchair weeps.

2. "As stocks continued to slide after markets opened, President
Trump is speaking at a $1
million dollar-a-person candlelight dinner Friday at Mar-a-Lago."

3. APD responded to report.
A transient stole 4 bags of cans
out of caller's vehicle parked
at the Chiropractor's office.

APD located subject who also had
a large trash can. Returned cans.
In custody. En route to jail.

4. "A new House Republican bill proposes significant cuts to the
Supplemental Nutrition
Assistance Program. potentially impacting millions of Americans
who rely on the program for
assistance."

5. a circus acrobat
was my grandfather
with his cane hobbling
to the mailbox fearing
no check this month

John Lewis
Martha Ellen Johnson

And after the grieving in whatever way,
march on. Forward we go, arm in arm.
Do not enter the fray on the battlefield
of the oppressors with the weapons of
violence, hate, fear. Enter with ours, the
weapons that lead to the higher rock.
Non-violence, love, compassion. Keep
our eyes on the prize. Fearless. Undaunted.
Hate, fear, violence may have their day.
They will not prevail. They will fall by the
wayside and tremble at the sight of
what love conquers clothed in simple
garb, slow walking across the bridge.

Woven Wonder
Luke McGuinniety

spin weave warp weft
forked silk splits the night sky
a spider's lightning loom

The Burning
Swapna Sanchita

We are waiting for phoenixes to rise
Hoards of them- an odyssey
Gold-red embers shaking off of their tail feathers
After all, we sit beside mountains of ash
Fresh, ready, raw...

We watched it all disappear
Prized possessions, objects- breakable, inflammable
Things?
Homes, lives, memories- childhood, old age, dreams!

Everything that meant something
All that we held so dear

And upon this graveyard
Upon this cremation ground
Of the priceless, we may someday begin to rebuild
Our ephemeral, tiny, apparently insignificant worlds
Haunted by the howling ghosts that will dance in flaming robes

But all that might be later - for tonight we keep vigil
Waiting for a birds shrieking
Waiting for its healing tears
Because ours seem to mean nothing
So many yesterdays that we sewed into tapestries
One thread at a time, so much time
Collecting, amassing
Putting each one in the perfect place
So that it may all come together in a wondrous mosaic.

Were we merely pretending we held it together?

Wondering....
Because that is all we can do - for now
Waiting for that wonderful thing with feathers

Waiting hopelessly, with nothing but hope
Until one of us, braver, stronger, wiser - gives up
On the infernal waiting
And walks towards the waters that lie uselessly
In swatches, besides these burning hills
Doing nothing, but lazily ebb, rise, ebb and rise again...

And maybe they will find ways
To split apart oceans and snatch away land
Land that is free of the stench of smoke
Where they grow marvelous mansions, erect edifices
And fill the spaces within the walls they raise
With laughter, with love.

And someone will sit at the window that lets in all the sunlight
And with singed fingers that hold a needle and thread
Embroider a terrible tale of resurrection
Into a silken piece cloth that waits
To capture in tiny pin pricks the past
So that tomorrow will see all that was lost
And remember,
So that tomorrow may know all that was remade
And remember.

line up
Joan McNerney

stand on one line to register
at a clinic showing your card
to see the medical on duty

sit and wait and wait and wait
until medical rushes in fast talk
handing you some prescription

pull out your checkbook
adding lines of figures
hoping to come out even

stand on a line marked exit
to pay for the visit which
takes checks cash or credit

drive away cautiously sure
never to cross over any
double yellow traffic lines

stand on winding line at
drug counter now paying
for an unknown medicine

stand on L O N G line to buy
something to eat unable
to decipher nutrition labels

make sure to line up your
car when you come home
carefully keeping it vertical

walk quickly down that
line of apartments
each door mud brown

this shows you follow the
straight and narrow in this
personal hell of lines

just yesterday
Joan McNerney

I thought there would be something pure to
hold close

can we ever have enough sweet moments
to keep?

or are we simply dark voices crying out in
wind storms?

buying despair on installment each hour pushing
another aside

sometimes it feels like my thoughts just fall
apart

far from this brutal world worthless as lost keys
broken windows

Thoughts from Within
Wayne Bebler

Inside myself I walk
Wandering
In my abyss
Wondering
Why
I can't find a path of
Understanding
I want
Just a few steps
To let me
Experience
A joyful sky
Or caressing waters
To have a soulful moment
With others
To enjoy the freedom
Of entanglements
That of giving hearts
And tears
Of expressing fears
For just seconds of cheers
I want to know
Not just see
The clouds in the mountains
I want to hear the whispers
Of wind
As I get free of my darkness

We Are Here
Sage Taylor Kingsley

We
Are
Here.

We are disabled and struggling to function We are
divergent minds racing voices shaking We are
single mothers and fathers We are underpartnered parents without
villages We are carless and
homeless We are over40s starting over post divorces and losses We
are oh-so-many shapes and
colors and isn't that fucking beautiful We are queer and trans and
grey and bi and straight and
very, very curious and we scoff at labels We are political
rabblerousers and activists and cynical
and yet hopeful We are spiritual crystal collectors and moon
worshippers tree huggers and sage
burners We are coupon cutters and business owners wage slaves and
consultants in suits We are
yogis and tantrikas cuddlers and chocolate lovers We are scientists
and engineers teachers and
preachers We are poets and dancers singers and baristas We are trust
fund babies doing good and
thrift store treasure hunters We are students and landladies flippers
and bridge builders We are
grandparents and waitresses gardeners and drivers We are visible
and invisible and above all
indivisible We are harmonizing and energizing reapprising and
above all we are mobilizing We
are everywhere
We are!
Here!

The Modern-Day Serenity Prayer
Sage Taylor Kingsley

Knowing the difference between:
"It is what it is"
and
"Oh, hell, no, time to kick some ass!"
is crucial if you want to enjoy your stay on Planet Earth.

Incident at the State Fair
Louise Moises

Northwestern New Jersey, fields of lush grassland
surrounded by dense forests, home to generations of farmers
who truck their livestock to the State Fair.
Friend of the family, he went to school with my daughter-in-law,
sits on bale of hay directing his four sons in the care
of his big black angus steers. The boys, as he calls them,
muck the stalls, fork hay, curry the massive cows,
lean affectionately against their flanks.

I'm introduced, the grandmother from California.
The sons wipe their hands on the legs of their jeans,
before extending them in firm, cordial shakes.
One smiles with a row of silver braces.
The father, pleased to meet me, rises and offers a hand,
then patiently answers my questions about cows and farming.
Behind him a locker displays blue, red and cream colored award
ribbons.

His prize steer won first place and has been sold.
Pride shows in the faces of his sons.
A slight breeze disturbs the dusty stalls,
blows the ribbons aside to reveal three identical decals:
> *Trump, Make America Great Again*
I catch my breath and hold my tongue.
As we walk away, my son says,
> *Good people, always helping folks, great family.*

Then I realize, perhaps for the first time,
> these folks are *not the enemy,*
> there is goodness in everyone.

I decline to unfriend
those who think differently than myself.

It's time for us to listen to each other.
Someone must enter the hay strewn stall,
offer a handshake before it's too late.

Art Project
Louise Moises

Today, my seven-year-old grandson declares, *Let's make happy signs!*
Under his direction, with pens, crayons, glue and stickers,
we create *happy signs*, one for each room of the house.

He begins with a drawing for his parent's bedroom—
a family group with the cat at their feet. All are smiling.
He lays the paper on the floor just inside the bedroom door.

For the kitchen he creates grinning broccoli, a laughing tomato,
a dozen small blue berries with dotted eyes and upturned mouths,
and a dancing strawberry. He hangs the sign on the fridge with magnets.

I sit next to him, encouraging his joyous project without lifting a pen.
We spend almost two hours of a late summer afternoon shoulder to shoulder.
He chats the entire time repeating *happy* dozens of times.

For the bathroom, he sketches a toilet with welcoming arms,
a jaunty step stool, and a bathtub filled with *happy* blue water.
He tapes the sign to the bathroom mirror.

The living room sign sports the grey sofa with laughing pillows,
television screen beaming with bright orange lips.
The table where he eats dinner holds only *happy* food.

For his own room, he draws a self-portrait smiling from ear to ear,
then draws a big circle around the border of the page.
The whole room is happy, he declares.

He doesn't end there, there's a sign for the car,
one for the back yard and one for the front.

And finally he says, *Dancing Grandma* (for that's what he calls me)
We need a happy sign for your motor home.
(I have driven across the country to be with this child)

Now he draws two large smiling figures,
me and my traveling companion cat, Grady.
Together we bring the *happy sign* to my RV.

If only he could draw *happy signs*
for all those places in the world
so much in need of his spirit.

Demons
Janet Martinez-Elliot

Not sure if I caught the monster or if they caught me.
All I know is that they are alive and breathing, somewhere hiding
and lurking.
I'm inexplicably drawn to those long crusty claws that pierce
through my peaceful realities.
Wielding shards of glassy dark reflections which stab my longing
heart,
Spinning through the cosmos I fall through galaxies suspended in
time.
Bouncing between worlds sprinkled with demons which remain
disturbingly familiar.

Is this the future or the end?
Am I truly flying free or being recaptured.
Wings clipped before rising to soar.
The opportunity to be blessed with gift of time and space to develop
my intellect and emotional maturity,
Only to slip back into the vile feelings of hatred, insecurities, and
discontent which permeate my current consciousness.
A necessary process I suppose.
Yet with each droplet that falls, burning my flesh with compassion
and love, will this pain truly heal what ails me?
 or
Just leave me with memorable scars of dreams unrealized for
generations?

Can the beauty I see in the longing eyes of strangers dwindle down
to this dilemma?
Effort or effortless.
Lucky or unlucky.
You can or you can't.
That monster's laser red eyes now slicing through my soul which
holds the balance of my perceived world.
Which truth will prevail?
Did I catch the monster or did they catch me?

They Come
Kathleen Herrmann

They come because they could not stay
Kim jumped into a ditch, bullets cracking round her
Ibrahim saw things that no child should ever see
Chuyu and her mother ran, chased by barbaric soldiers
Hanibal disappeared, held for ransom
Zeena drifted for days in an overcrowded boat
Yulia's mother barred the door against thugs and threats
They leave because they cannot stay, grieving the land that once yielded to their
 footfalls, the scented air that skimmed their cheeks, that unmatched shade of

sky

blue

They come with open wounds and sealed lips
Kim picks raspberries, studies calculus
Ibrahim wants to be a model
Chuyu does not know if she can make it here
Hanibal likes his privacy
Zeena wishes for connection, faces rejection
Yulia loves new school, new friends
They come as family, only to be branded as drug dealers, criminals, rapists,
 to hide, to risk deportation to nowhere
So this is America

I Was Never Afraid of FEMA

Jacalyn Eyvonne

We are caught in real-life horror.
When nature decides to shake up our dreams.
But I was never afraid of FEMA
Not when the wind slices roofs as it screams
When the levees broke and water spilled over
city streets, or when the skylines darkened
above fiery glows, or when the ground
split open beneath our feet.
Yet, I've never been afraid of the people
Who showed up with hope and something to eat.

I was never afraid of the air testers, the water checkers,
or those making sure my children can breathe.
Or the scientists who seek the cures
before sickness brings me to my knees
I'm not afraid of the healers, the helpers
Those who seek to protect our lives.
But I am afraid of the new script being written,
as horror drips from the daily headlines.
Politicians slash our safety nets,
Gut departments that once protected and helped,
Chaos has become the biggest winner.
Progress is the fear of many.
Our air and water are sold to the highest bidder
As sickness is allowed to run wild in our streets.
The suit-wearers call it policy. I call it sabotage.
The rewriting of all our protections
To slowly destroy all our lives.

I was never afraid of FEMA
The helpers. Healers. Protectors
I was never afraid of the big yellow bird, PBS or NPR, either
The scariest part of this movie is something we must
all understand. The monster no longer resides outside our house
It sleeps beside us next to our bed.

BIOS

Abigail Brown: Thirty-one-year-old Abigail Brown is from Omaha, Nebraska. Poetry is her form of passion.

Alex Burton began writing poetry with his girlfriend, Kristian Baisac, during his senior year of high school. What started as a single creative project quickly grew into a meaningful pursuit as they both discovered how much they enjoyed the process. Over time, they continued to write together, and Alex loves it.

Alyza Lee Salomon resides in Hercules, California, and has been dancing with Natica Angilly's Poetic Dance Theater Company since 2003. She earned her M.A. in English Lit. from Sonoma State, where she fell in love with the writing of Virginia Woolf. Her poems have appeared in local anthologies and online.

Amana Mission is a word-jazz technician and synthesist with Air Lift Underground. She moonlights as a concept-juggler and thought-bomb engineer in the People's Imperial Army of Clowns and daylights as a horticulturist.

Amanda Fall, creator of The Phoenix Soul online community, is an intuitive artist, writer, and creative encourager. You can find her wandering the old-growth forest behind her home in Oregon, notebook in hand, or beach-combing at ocean's edge. Amanda's guided journal, Messy Beautiful You, is available on Amazon.

Amusa Yusuf Owolabi was born in Ghana. He is a Nigerian. He is a budding writer and has masters in Theatre Art from the University of Ibadan, Nigeria. His writings have appeared in several journals and he has a flair for writing.

Andrena Zawinski's poetry is known for social concern. *Born Under the Influence* is her fourth full-length poetry collection. Poems appeared in *CQ, Evening Street, Tule Review, Pinyon*, and anthologies *Light on the Wall of Life, Raising Lily Ledbetter, Crossing Class, Fire & Rain Eco Poetry of CA,* and others.

Angelica Blyden was born in Philadelphia and is now based in the Bay Area. Angelica began writing poetry at 13 after a teacher gifted her a journal. An early performer on the Voices in Power stage, she weaves memory and prophecy, stitching together legacy, love, and survival through er multidisciplinary artistry.

Anne M Carson is an independent researcher, creative writing teacher, essayist and awarded poet, living on the unceded Bunurong Country in Australia. Her fifth poetry collection, *George Sand (and Me: a poetic biography,* will be published in 2026. Her PhD (2023, RMIT) received an Outstanding Dissertation Prize (AERA 2024).

Astraia Rodriguez resides in South Texas with their cats and domestic partner, attempting to write while working full-time in a capitalist world that demands productivity, not creativity. Writing about past traumas and events, Astraia attempts to make sense of the world around them through writing and poetry.

Audrey T. Williams, MFA is a Black American woman with South Asian heritage. She is a poet, writer, and literary arts organizer bridging speculative literature with ancestral wisdom and earth-honoring practices. Named inaugural Speculative Poet-in-Residence at BayCon 2025, she is Co-Chair for the World Fantasy Convention 2026 in Oakland. Founder of AncestralFutures.org, her work appears in *Lightspeed Magazine, Space & Time*, and *Conjuring Worlds*: *An Afrofuturist Textbook,* among others. Through "Words for Wellness" workshops, Williams transforms the literary arts into a radical practice of resilience, exploring ancestral archetypes and the preservation of cultural narratives through imagination as a means of collective liberation.

Becky Bishop White is an award-winning poet whose work has appeared in numerous anthologies, including several published by Moonstone Press. She and author James W. White live in a waterside town near San Francisco Bay and share a life filled with love, books, art, and wonderful family and friends.

Beverly Al-Kareem. I have been writing since I was a little girl. Once I learned to read words, they became my passion. Using them in creating a poem was the highlight of my dream as I struggled with abandonment. After attending Grambling College, I learned that using words was a means of communication. I was able to expand my vocabulary, which opened many opportunities for me today. I write Poetry to express myself, to use the tools to inspire and uplift others. Poetry is my passion; my books illustrate that.

Brandon Vu is an educator in the Bay Area. His work has appeared in *KQED, Ghost City Review*, and *The San Franciscan*. He has a mother named Julie and a cat named Raymond.

Cassandra M Walton (Poetry Lady) is a requested -- sought-after poetic performer in the nation. Local DJs call her the "Bay Area's Best Kept Secrets"; that is, until the release of her vibrant CD(s) "Love According To Love" and "Born To Climb" and her latest release "The Vinyl Collection - New Dawn, New Day". The Lady, Her Music, Her Poetry, Poems and Songs, are heard on the airways throughout the United States, and internationally.

Christie Lessman - Hailing from America's heartland, Christie Lessman channels her creative spirit into poetry, lyrics, and uplifting words that resonate with her audience.

Clare Olivares is a California painter and poet living in the San Francisco Bay Area. Her work has been published in literary journals including *The Plentitudes, Borderline Press, Star82 Review, Remington Review, Juste Milieu, samfiftyfour,* and *Fatal Flaw.* Olivares' writing reflects daily observations of living with grace and curiosity.

Cleo Griffith has been widely published in journals such as *Main Street Rag, Westward Quarterly,* and *Straylight.* She has been on the editorial staff of the poetry quarterly, *Song of the San Joaquin,* since it began in 2003.

Connie Cyndi Chu is a self-published author of mostly science fiction and fantasy. She is also a poet on many topics that tickle her fancy.

Susan H. Evans lives in Baltimore, Maryland, and enjoys writing poetry, memoirs, and creative nonfiction. She has been published in many online and print magazines, journals, and anthologies.

Dan MBO KUBA is a contributing editor with a background in Finance and Development, having been part of the Commercial, Marketing, and Administrative School. He carries out his freelance tasks as an SEO writer with various writing options with various firms and establishments. Author of several Books and articles, notably for the *Revue Avenir* and the Revue of the digitalization and the management. Since 2016, he has been working as an Author, participating in various related activities.

Daniel Miltz, A poet at heart since his formative, bohemian years in California, he draws enduring inspiration from the raw energy and spontaneous voice of the Beat Generation. His poetic journey has garnered over 1,600 accolades across international poetry forums, and his work has appeared in more than 250 anthologies worldwide.

Dianna MacKinnon Henning taught through California Poets in the Schools, received California Arts Council grants, taught poetry workshops through the William James Association's Prison Arts Program, including Folsom Prison, Diamond View Middle School and now runs "The Thompson Peak Writers' Workshop." Publications, in part: *Women in a Golden State,* 2025; Visions 2025; *The Power of the Feminine,* Vol. II 2024; *One Art Poetry,* 2024; *Folkways Press; Mocking Heart Review,* 2024; *Poet News,* and more, including Nine nominations for a Pushcart. MFA Vermont College of Fine Arts. https://diannahenning.com

Dina Oraz Dinara Orazbekova (creative pseudonym Dina Oraz) - poet, writer, translator, journalist, actor, public figure, head of the creative association "AVANGARD," vice-president of the ICPD. Born in Kokshetau, lives in Astana, Republic of Kazakhstan. Author of Children's books *Who treats lions' teeth?, Where does the unicorn live?* And what's *my name?*

Elizabeth Greene has published four books of poetry, most recently *No Ordinary Days* (Ekstasis, 2024), and a novel, *A Season Among Psychics* (Inanna, 2018). She lives in Kingston, Ontario, Canada on the unceded territory of the Anishnaabe, Haudenosaunee and Huron-Wendat.

Elizabeth Vrenios' award-winning chapbook about the loss of her son in the Pan Am 103 Crash, *Special Delivery*, was published in 2016, *Empty the Ocean with a Thimble* in 2021, and her latest full-length collection, *A Concerto for an Empty Frame* in 2023. Her fourth, (Ra ven) is forthcoming this year. Nominated for a Pushcart, and Best of Net several times, she has poems published in numerous anthologies and journals, is Professor Emerita from American University, and has been the editor of the Writers of Mendocino County anthology for several years.

Emma Alexis Woodard is occasionally the name of our poet. She has a lot to say, but has no idea how to say it, so it comes out in various shades of anger and sadness in prose. She's 32, a west coaster, and a double Aquarius. Emma Woodard doesn't have a favorite or least favorite thing about herself. She's a big proponent of eating your waffles slightly burnt with creamy peanut butter. There aren't many impressions she does well, but she does a startlingly astute impression of a 30-something with their life together. Maybe she's born with it, maybe it's Fluoxetine.

Evie Groch's memoirs, poems, and short stories have been published in the *New York Times, The SF Chronicle, The Contra Costa Times, The Journal*, in various anthologies, and online. She is President of the Ina Coolbrith Circle (Poetry) and writes of travel, languages, immigration, and justice in *Half the Hurricanes*.

Faleeha Hassan, Pulitzer Prize and Pushcart Prize Nomination. Member of IWA and Who's Who in America, Cultural Ambassador, Iraq, USA, winner of the Women's Excellence award, winner of the Grand Jury Award of the SAHITTO, one of the Excellence selection committees, winner of the Women's Arts Award. SAHITTO AWARD JUDGING PANEL. Winner of the HerStory Award from Women's Federation for World Peace, New Jersey 2024, Cultural Ambassador - Iraq, USA, and Winner of the Naji Naaman Literary Prize 2025.

Gabriella Garofalo, born in Italy some decades ago, Gabriella Garofalo fell in love with the English language at six, started writing poems (in Italian) at six, and is the author of these books *Lo sguardo di Orfeo; L'inverno di vetro; Di altre stelle polari; Casa di erba; Blue Branches; A Blue Soul, After The Blue Rush.*

Gail Newman, a child of Holocaust survivors, was raised in a community of Jewish immigrants in Los Angeles. Her poems have appeared in journals and anthologies including *Nimrod International, Prairie Schooner, The Bellingham Review, Ghosts of the Holocaust*. A collection of poetry, *One World* was published by Moon Tide Press. *Blood Memory*, chosen by Marge Piercy for the Marsh Hawk Press Poetry Prize, won the Northern California Authors and Publishers Gold Award for Poetry and the Best Book Awards Winner in the Religious category. Gail lives in San Francisco and Sebastopol, California.

Gail Wasserman is a poet/ lyricist from California. Gail serves on the Board of Benicia Literary Arts and has several publications in the *Benicia Herald*, Moonstone Arts Center, Read and Green Books Press, the *Chelsea Underground*, and numerous other anthologies. In addition, Gail received Honorable Mention in the Ina Coolbrith 2022 and 2023 Poetry Contests as well as Third Prize with the Dancing Poets in 2025.

Hanh Chau - Hanh is from San Jose, CA. In her spare time, she enjoys poetry writing, listening to music, and ballroom dancing. She has worked for Kaiser Permanente as a patient care services representative for 20 years.

Hilary King. Originally from the Blue Ridge Mountains of Virginia, Hilary King is now a poet living in the San Francisco Bay Area of California. Her poems have appeared in *Ploughshares, TAB, Salamander, Belletrist,* and other publications. Her book *Stitched on Me* was published by Riot in Your Throat Press in 2024.

Isaac Aju is a Nigerian poet whose works focus on social justice and security. He has appeared in US and UK literary journals.

Jacob R. Moses is a poet, spoken word artist, and educator from New York City. He penned the full-length poetry book, Grimoire (iiPublishing, 2021). Currently, he is an adjunct professor at Wagner College.

James Quinn, born in Vallejo and raised in Benicia, has roots in both Mexican and American cultures. He's a schoolteacher who's been lighting up the classroom for over a decade. With an impressive 11-year run in teaching elementary and middle school students, James started his journey at the Elmer Cave Language Academy in Vallejo, teaching third graders. Nowadays, you'll find him inspiring minds over in Mountain View. In his spare time, James enjoys writing poetry. Much of his work centers around the human condition.

Jan Wiezorek writes from southwestern Michigan and walks regularly along McCoy Creek Trail. He is the author of the poetry chapbook *Prayer's Prairie* (Michigan Writers Cooperative Press) and the forthcoming chapbook *Forests of Woundedness* (Seven Kitchens Press). Wiezorek's poetry has appeared in *The London Magazine*, *Vita Poetica*, and *BlazeVOX*. Visit janwiezorek.substack.com.

Janet Martinez-Eliot has lived in Vallejo, California for about 10 years. A community arts activist, she puts on a free pop-up microcinema featuring shorts by underrepresented filmmakers during the Vallejo Art Walks with her husband, David. "I started out writing my husband a love poem for his birthday every year since we met. My fascination with poetry and the poet community in Vallejo has grown, and I'm currently writing more and learning to read my poems in public with the support of local poets."

Jeff Kingman's poetry collection, *Beyond That Hill I Gather*, was published by Finishing Line Press in 2021. His chapbook, *On A Road*, was published in 2019. He is the winner of the 2018 Eyelands Book Award (Greece) for an unpublished poetry book, a finalist in the 2018 Hillary Gravendyk Prize book competition, and was long listed for the 2025 ONLY POEMS Poet of the Year Prize. He has been published in PANK,

Clackamas, Action Spectacle, and others. Jeff has a Master's degree in Music Composition and has played drums in rock bands most of his life.

Jennifer Sweeney is a photographer and poet with an MFA in Studio Art from the University of Galway in association with the Burren College of Art in Ireland and a BFA in Photography from Parsons School of Design in NYC. Jennifer currently lives and works in New Jersey.

Jerome Gagnon is the author of *Rumors of Wisdom* and *Refuge for Cranes.* An alumnus of San Francisco State University, he lives in Alameda County.

Joan McNerney's poetry is published worldwide in over forty countries in numerous literary magazines. Four Best of the Net nominations have been awarded to her. Her books *The Muse in Miniature, Love Poems for Michael I & II, At Work*, and *Light & Shadows* are all available at Amazon.com

Johanna Ely is the author of four poetry books, *Transformation, Tides of the Heart–Poems for Benicia, Postcards from a Dream* (Blue Light Press 2020), and *What Still Matters* (Last Laugh Productions 2023). She has also co-authored a book with three other women poets titled, *Love's Meditation* (Random Lane Press 2023). Johanna served as the sixth poet laureate of Benicia, California, and is a board member of the Ina Coolbrith Circle of Poets, one of the oldest poetry groups in California.

Jonathan Watson is a law librarian in California. He received his B.A. in English from UC Berkeley, M.A. in English from CSUS, and MLIS from SJSU (he and his mother Jo-Ann graduated together). His poetry appears in *Avatar Review, Sacramento Literary Review, Forum Magazine, Carquinez Review, Edition III, eMerge Magazine* and the book *Peacocks & Poems: A Fusion of Poetry, Art, and Music.*

Julie Voice is an educator, writer, author, publisher, poet, publicist, community builder, and mother who resides in her hometown of Vallejo, CA. A self-taught, self-published, trademarked artist and producer known for her local events and holistic approach to wellness, Serial Muse™ embodies her poetic vision. Writing allows her to explore the human experience and heal through creative expression. Among her published works are a series of three poetry art books, *Serial Muse Chronicles*, and her latest work, *Forthcoming*, now available on Amazon. She invites you to discover the unseen web of life through her writing.

Katrina (Kathy) Monroe is the current Benicia Poet Laureate, who runs a program of monthly Open Mics, workshops on topics of interest, a series of Ekphrastic readings, special poetry events, a national Love Poetry Contest, workshops with kids, and a poetry scholarship program. A lifelong lover of language, she enjoys experimenting with a variety of styles, with her favorite topics being character studies, nature, relationships, social justice, and topography. Her work has resulted in several prizes, journal publications, and the chapbook *Transitions and Reinventions*. Her next publication is a collection of poems on her canine loves, *Having the Last Woof!*

Kristian Baisac is a first-year student at the University of Richmond. She began her poetic journey with Poetry Out Loud (POL), where she became the Solano County Champion and competed in the California competition during her senior year at Fairfield High School. With a love of learning and dedication, she was the valedictorian and is a recipient of the Gates Scholarship. Since POL, she has been writing poetry for personal fulfillment, whether shared through local ekphrastic events or crafted for self-expression.

Krzysztof T. Babrowski's books are available in the USA, Spain, Chile, India, Canada, and more. And include titles such as *The Element of Unpredictability* (2024, Alien Buddha Press), *Die Anomalie* (2020, Der Romankiosk), *Escape* (2025, Wolf Books Publishing), and numerous others. https://www.facebook.com/Krzysztof.Dabrowski.pisarz

Lalit Kumar writes a regular column on adventure and travel in 'India Currents magazine'. He is the author of two poetry books, 'Yosemite of my Heart' and 'Years Spent - Exploring Poetry in Adventure, Life and Love.' His works have appeared in various Anthologies, including *Our California*. Find him on Instagram at @lalitk06 or www.lalitkumaronline.com

Linda Garing. After raising three children and now the grandmother of five, my husband and I are living vibrantly in an over-55 community. Our Poetry Group meets monthly: we write, we read, we share the rich tapestry of thoughts that become our poems, and we feel hopeful.

Louise Moises is an award-winning poet whose chapbook *Peace Is a Pelican* is available from Finishing Line Press. She travels solo in her RV, driving cross-country to absorb the vast diversity of our country and its people. Louise writes poems daily, inspired by her travels.

Luke McGuinniety is 66 years and going strong - a criminal lawyer in HK - here for the simple joy of being alive and vain enough to wish to share his thoughts with all.

Lynn Carole Brown is an emerging poet/writer who has been published in the *Missouri Humanities Magazine* Winter 2024 edition, for her poem titled, *River Rats*. In addition, her poetry has been published as part of a Cupertino community anthology titled *Celebrate Creativity*.

Lynn White lives in North Wales. Her work is influenced by issues of social justice, events, places, and people she has known or imagined. She is especially interested in exploring the boundaries of dreams, fantasy, and reality. She has been nominated for Pushcarts, Best of the Net, and a Rhysling Award. https://lynnwhitepoetry.blogspot.com and https://www.facebook.com/Lynn-White-Poetry-1603675983213077/

Maiah A Merino, a first and second-generation Mexican American/Chicana Poet, has work forthcoming in *Cascadia Zen and Weeping Women: The Haunting Presence of La Llorona in Mexican and Chicanx Lore*. Maiah guest co-edited The Yellow Medicine Review's Spring 2022, Journal titled: *Miracles & Defining Moments*, was a recent contributor to *I Sing the Salmon Home: Poems from Washington State* and has poems in The Yellow Medicine Review. She was a 2021/2022 "Writing the Land Poet" and recipient of the 2021 Artist Trust GAP Award.

Martha Ellen is a retired social worker living on the Oregon coast. MFA. Poems and prose have been published in various journals and online forums. She writes to process the events of her life.

Mary Susan Gast is a poet, theologian, human rights advocate, and musician. As she ages, she finds it increasingly difficult and immaterial to differentiate among those identities. She became Benicia's 8th Poet Laureate just as COVID descended. Mary Susan continues to edit the newspaper column *Going The Distance,* launched in 2020, bringing together writings that offer strength, hope, and solidarity in unsettled times.

Matt J McGee writes in Thousand Oaks, CA. In 2024, his work appeared in *Four Feathers, Last Stanza*, and *Non-Binary Review*. When not typing, he drives around in rented cars and plays goalie in local hockey leagues.

Md. Nuruddin Pier Shihab is a Bangladeshi poet and lecturer in English at R. P. Shaha University. His poetry, published on various literary platforms, explores the themes of identity, conflict, and human experience, earning recognition in competitions. Beyond poetry, he has authored research articles and book chapters on literature and culture.https://rpsu.ac.bd/faculty/md-nuruddin-pier-shihab

Melody Anderson-Brumidis is a Vallejo poet. Her wife of 39 years, Loretta, is her rock. She is active in the Solano poetry world. Her family, five kids, three grandchildren, six chihuahuas, and a calico cat–provides material for her poetry. She enjoys gardening, walking her dogs, and reading Donna Leon mysteries.

Michael New studied with James T. Farrell and served as managing editor of *Country Gentleman* magazine. He taught writing, including poetry, to sixth graders in Vallejo until retiring. His work has appeared in the *Saturday Evening Post, The Thieving Magpie, Ultramarine Literary Review*, and *Wayne Literary Review*. Addison-Wesley published his book *The Year of the Apple*. He writes a monthly column for the *Crockett Signal* and recently began resurrecting stories from his personal archives—work written years ago about events that shaped him even earlier.

Monique Rardin Richardson (Tri-Valley Branch) is a poet, photographer, and author of the award-winning memoir *When Then Became Now* and poetry chapbook *Pieces of Me,* and has had poems appear in several anthologies and online publications, including Viewless Wings Publisher and the *Havik Journal of Art and Literature*. Her photos and artwork have been featured in galleries across the United States, including the 2023 Open Show at the de Young Museum in San Francisco. To learn more about Monique, you can visit her at moniquerardinrichardson.com

Murray Eiland (born in Vallejo) is a poet and archaeologist.

Nafia Dawn participates in poetry readings in and around Solano County, California. She considers poetry a tool for healing, using her voice to advocate for human rights and wellbeing.

Oliver sopulu odo is a Nigerian writer. He studied English and literary studies/Theatre and film studies at the University of Nigeria Nsukka. He was longlisted in The Green We Left Behind short story competition, the spectrum Poetry Anthology competition, and the Engaging Borders Africa short story competition. He was one of the winners in the Kepressng Anthology competition (Rebirth). *Decolonial passage* Literary magazine, Best of the Net nominee. And elsewhere.

Oseni Abdullateef Babatunde is a Nigerian writer, teacher, and researcher from Oyo State, Nigeria. He holds a bachelor's and master's degree in English and is currently pursuing his Ph.D. in the same field. He is a passionate poet and researcher; he has written both creative and academic works, many of which have been published in books and journals. For Oseni, poetry is more than an art form; it is a way to understand life and build bridges between people. He is driven by a love for learning, a commitment to sharing knowledge, and a belief in the transformative power of words.

Paul Lobo Portugés teaches creative writing at UCSB, taught at UC Berkeley, USC, and the University of Provence. Books include *Sorrow and Hope, Breaking Bread, The Visionary Poetics of Allen Ginsberg, Saving Grace, Hands Across the Earth, The Flower Vendor, Paper Song, Aztec Birth, The Body Electric Journal, The Bullet Had His Face in the Soul of His Blood, The Silent Spring of Rachel Carson, Ginsberg: On Tibetan Buddhism, Mantras, Drugs, Witness*, and *Falling Short.*

R. K. Singh has published poems, articles, and book reviews in various magazines and journals over the years and taught English for Science and Technology and Indian Writing in English at IIT-ISM, Dhanbad, for nearly four decades. His latest books of poems include *Poems and Micropoems* (2023), Knocking *Vistas And Other Poems* (2024), and *Leaves of Silence* (2025). More at https://pennyspoetry.fandom.com/wiki/R.K._Singh

Sage Taylor Kingsley is a romantic mystic poet who wordsmiths as an editor/ghostwriter at Reedsy and SageforYourPage.com. Dive into her pool of wordlove on Substack and in her debut collection (finally! at age 60): Beautiful Late Bloomer: Passionate Poetry and Mystic Musings. A poet since 1974, Sage penned 1,300 poems since 2021, some featured in *Orange is Not a Color: Poems Against Totalitarianism; Embraced by the Divine; Self-Caring; We'Moon,* and other magical places. An escapee from Queens, Sage lives in the Bay Area, where she writes about sacred relationships, motherhood, self-love, nature, mindfulness/heartfulness, and aging with feist and grace. substack.com/@sagepoetess

Sam Hendrian is a Los Angeles-based filmmaker, poet, and playwright striving to foster empathy through art. From writing personalized poems for passersby outside of LA's oldest independent bookstore every Sunday to making Chaplin-esque silent films about loneliness and human connection once a month, Sam lives to make other people feel seen and validated. More poems and films can be found on Instagram at @samhendrian143.

Sharon Pretti lives in San Francisco, California. Her work has appeared in *Calyx, The MacGuffin, ONE ART, The Bellevue Literary Review, Canary*, and elsewhere. She's received multiple Pushcart Prize nominations and was selected for the Best New Poets 2024 anthology. Sharon is a retired medical social worker and, for many years, she had the pleasure of teaching poetry workshops in nursing homes and assisted living facilities in the San Francisco Bay Area. Visit her at sharonpretti.com

Shawna L. Swetech is a retired hospital nurse, is a poet and artist. Her poetry appears in *Rattle, The Healing Muse, Ars Medica, Pulse*, and the *American Journal of Nursing*, among others. Her work, ranging from the personal to the political, draws from the deep wells of human nature and the natural world. Shawna is a co-host for the monthly reading series, Rivertown Poets. Her first poetry collection, *Standing In Their Fire*, based on her nursing career, will be published in late summer 2025 by Kelsay Books. Shawna believes poetry and art are important medicines for the ills of our modern world.

Dr. Shilpa Chakravarty has been working as a medical writer for a couple of years before she took to freelance content creation. She has worked for several publication houses, in preparing book chapters, questionnaires, and study materials. She has attained her Doctoral degree in Science from the University of Allahabad (India). Of late, writing poems has become her favorite form of expression.

Shirley Smothers is an amateur Writer, Poet, and Artist. She mostly writes short stories. Some of her short stories can be viewed at Shirleysmothers@storystar.com. Last year, she self-published her second book. This book can be found at ShirleysmothersSolasta@pothi.com. She was chosen as Artist of the Month, June 2025, Glomag Submissions, Facebook.

Souad Zakarani, Moroccan Poetess & Translator. Her first publication by the BRENTANO GESELLSCHAFT was quite an experience that improved her writing process. She writes in four languages and develops a style that blends traditional form and aesthetics with contemporary sensibilities, always striving to find the extraordinary in the ordinary. Anthologies in Austria, Germany & Spain: *Whispers across Language*s by Barcelona Adabia. - Frühlings Anthologie 2025' beim Thomas Opfermann - *Im Fadenkreuz der Archetypen, Märchen, Sex & Gende*r beim Wiener Verlag. - Lyrischer Lorbeer'24,"Regenbogeninsel"Anthology. - Four times successful publication of contemporary poetry in the Brentano Gesellschaft Frankfurter Bibliothek.

Susan H. Evans lives in Baltimore, Maryland, and enjoys writing poetry, memoir, and creative nonfiction. She is published in many online and print magazines, journals, and anthologies.

Susan Kelly-DeWitt is a former Wallace Stegner Fellow and the author of *Frangible Operas*, (Gunpowder Press, 2024), *Gatherer's Alphabet* (Gunpowder Press, CA Poets Prize, 2022), *Gravitational Tug* (Main Street Rag, 2020), *Spider Season* (Cold River Press, 2016), *The Fortunate Islands* (Marick Press, 2008) and several previous small press collections. For more information, please visit www.susankelly-dewitt.com.

Suzanne Bruce- Fairfield Poet Laureate July 1, 2022 - December 31, 2024. Her poems have won several prizes and publication credits include *International Literary Quarterly, Copperfield Review, Suisun Valley Review, and California Quarterly.* Her books are *Voices Beyond the Canvas*, and *Her Visions Her Voices.* www.suzannebrucepoet.com

Swapna Sanchita is a poet, a storyteller and an educator. She is the author of five children's books and a poetry collection, Des Vu. Swapna shares some of her work on Instagram @sanchitaswapna and loves chocolate, coffee, and books, not necessarily in that order.

Tammy Smith is a poet and licensed clinical social worker based in Fair Lawn, New Jersey. She spent a significant part of her life in San Francisco, an experience that enriched her perspective and informs her poetic voice. With both professional and lived experience in mental health, her poetry explores the intersections of personal and collective struggle. Her poems have appeared in *Grand Little Things, Merion West, New Verse News, Eunoia Review, Synkroniciti, Poem Alone, Verse-Virtual*, and other literary journals.

Tezozomoc is a Los Angeles Chicano Essayist, Poet and 2009 Oscar Nominated Activist, internationally published and has been published by Amoxcalco Books for *I am not your Chihuahua*, and by Floricanto Press, *Gashes!: Poems and Pain from the halls of injustice*, a collection of poetry, 5/2025, shortlisted for the 2021-2025 international Beverly Prize Literary prize, 9/2019. Featured nationally and internationally across Zoom open virtual mics.

Tim Kahl [http://www.timkahl.com] [https://soundcloud.com/tnklbnny] is the author of six books of poems, most recently *Omnishambles (*Bald Trickster, 2019), *California Sijo* (Bald Trickster, 2022) *and Drips, Spills, Bursts, Tangles, and Washes* (Cold River Press, 2024). He is also an editor of *Clade Song* [http://www.cladesong.com]. He builds flutes, plays them and plays guitars, ukuleles, charangos and cavaquinhos as well. He currently teaches at California State University, Sacramento, where he sings lieder while walking on campus between classes.

Valdez Hill is a classical pianist, poet, and graphic designer. He has served on the Board of Directors for the Young People's Symphony Orchestra in Berkeley, CA. Valdez's poems, such as *Leda and the Swan: A Symphony of Sound and Fear* and *To the Night Stars,* have been published by Moonstone Arts Center and Verseve.

Virginia Barrett is a poet, writer, artist, editor, and educator. She earned her MFA in Writing from the University of San Francisco in 2016, where she was poetry editor of *Switchback.* Her seventh book of poetry, *The Vessels We Carry Keep Us Alive*, is forthcoming from Saint Julian Press. Her latest editing project, *BLUE: a Hue Are You* anthology, the second volume in a series, has just been released from Jambu Press. www.virginiabarrett.com

Vivien Cook is a poet based in Oakland. The genesis of *Reuters: Some of the Partisans Were Women* is derived from the last sentence of a news article where the journalist seemed write the words as an afterthought. *Long Distance Hiker Gone for Months: Kodak* is written for her son, who has logged over 8,000 miles to date.

Walid Abdallah is an Egyptian poet, author, and translator. His poetry and translations have appeared in international journals and anthologies. He has published several poetry collections and teaches English and comparative literature at Suez University, Egypt, exploring cross-cultural and existential themes in modern literature.

Wayne Bebler. Roland Wayne Bebler grew up on the Jersey Shore. He currently lives in North Carolina. He has lived throughout the United States, including the San Francisco Bay area, while working for USAir. His poetry has been published in the United States, the United Kingdom, and Nigeria.

Woody Shiflett is the engineer geek/business guy who hides out as an unlikely poet on occasion. He has been rewarded for this by having a number of poems published and winning awards at the Solano County Fair.

Zach Beach, MA, MS, AMFT, is a spiritual teacher, best-selling author, poet, therapist, intimacy coach, founder of The Heart Center love school, and host of The Learn to Love Podcast. Learn more at www.zachbeach.com.